Father Missed His Plane

A Memoir

BY

VINCENT LEE

Copyright © 2017 Vincent Lee
The right of Vincent Lee to be identified as the author of the work has been asserted by him in accordance with the Copyright, Designs and Patents Act, 1988.

All rights reserved. No part of this book may be reproduced or transmitted in any form or by any means, electronic or mechanical, including photocopying, recording or by any information storage and retrieval system, without written permission from the author, except in the case of a reviewer, who may quote brief passages embodied in critical articles or in a review.

Front Cover Picture courtesy of the author
Interior Pictures courtesy of the author

ISBN 978-0-9925939-1-9 (Paperback)

ISBN 978-0-9925939-0-2 (ebook edition)

First edition, February 2017

Contents
Author's Note
My Family Tree
Dedication
Prologue
Map of Cambodia

Humble Beginnings
It Ended Even Before It Began
Father Missed His Plane
The Long March
A Fork in the Road
Angkar Padevat
From Zero to Nothing
Boys Labour Camp
The Meeting
Borrowed Graves
Three Tons Per Hectare
Angkar Preparing Our Own Grave
The Thirteen Survivors
Revenge Always On Their Mind
Returning Home
7 - 3 = 4
Father's Last Advice
The Great Escape
Life in Khao-I-Dang Refugee Camp
Freedom Came at a Price
To Paris or Not To Paris
To The Land of Oz

Epilogue
Acknowledgements
About the Author

Author's Note

In those four years under the Khmer Rouge regime from 1975 to 1979, and two years thereafter, I had no access to a clock nor a calendar to identify and record the dates, months or years when events happened. I have tried the best I can to place my story in a chronological order using the monsoon seasons as guidance for my readers. The story is based on my own childhood memories, and mine alone, although some events in the village of Kor which are important to this story were recounted to me by my mother.

My Family Tree

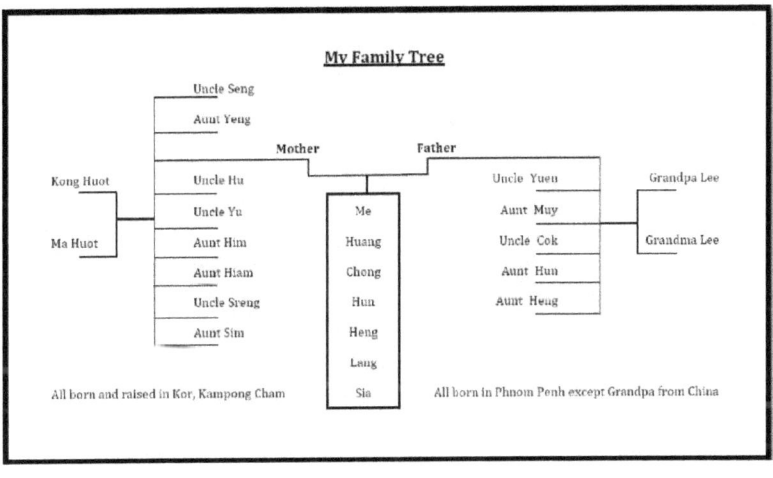

Dedication

To the three women in my life:

Grandma Lee: Thank you for giving me a renewed freedom.

My Mother: You do know everything.

Yuko, my wife, thank you for your love and support.

To all the refugees around the world, past, present and future, there is no place like home.

"When elephants collide, the ants get trampled"
Cambodian Proverb

When power falls into the wrong hands;
When a misguided intention is allowed full reign without consequence;
When concepts like "freedom" and "knowledge" are twisted by those of privilege:
Victims are the innocent.

PROLOGUE

Cambodia was once part of the great Khmer empire. The kingdom extended beyond its present-day borders west to include a section of Thailand, north to encompass a major portion of Laos and south to Vietnam, incorporating part of the Mekong Delta, known to Cambodian people as Khmer Krom (Lower Cambodia). Angkor Wat was the capital. Over the centuries there were countless conflicts and border disputes between Cambodia and Thailand, and Cambodia and Vietnam. The people of Thailand insisted that the ancient capital, Angkor Wat, belonged to them. The Vietnamese laid claim over the Mekong Delta, the Kingdom's biological treasure-trove. In the long history of fighting between Cambodia and her neighbours, however, nothing caused as much trauma and destruction to my country as what it experienced at the hands of the revolutionaries who were known as the Khmer Rouge from 1975 to 1979.

The region of Southeast Asia, later known as Indochina, which included Cambodia, Laos and Vietnam, had become a French protectorate in 1893. These three nations gained a brief independence from France when they were ruled by Japan during the Second World War, but once hostilities ceased French colonialism returned. This time, however, a new ideology was brewing in Asia: communism. It came to the fore in China after Chairman Mao's Communist Party defeated Chiang Kai-Shek's Kuomintang (the Chinese Nationalist Party) and established the People's Republic of China in Tiananmen Square, Beijing, on October 1, 1949. At around the same time, the Vietnamese Communist Party, (the Viet Minh), led by Ho Chi Minh, proclaimed the independence of Vietnam and had gained control of the northern half of the country by September 1945. France resisted the loss of her territories in the First Indochinese War until 1954. Because of fears Cambodia might ally itself with the Viet Minh to fight the colonial oppressor, Cambodian independence was granted on

November 9, 1953. Norodom Sihanouk initially assumed the dual roles of King and Prime Minister, but two years later in 1955, he abdicated the throne, although everyone in Cambodia still referred to him as the King Father.

As a result of the connection with France, many Cambodians could go and study in Paris. During this period, some embraced Marxism, and once they returned home in the mid-1950s, they began to organize their own political parties. Among them was a man who later became known as Pol Pot.

The Cold War was in full swing by this time. The USA and the USSR were at loggerheads, and the fear of all Southeast Asia falling to communism gripped America. As Prime Minister, Prince Sihanouk pledged to keep Cambodia neutral during the 1954 Geneva Conference but refused to join SEATO - the Southeast Asia Treaty Organisation. One intention of SEATO was to block communism making further inroads into Asia and to fight against the North Vietnamese. By the late sixties, the Vietnam War was well underway. Inevitably armies from both sides spilled over the border into Cambodia. America wanted Cambodia's approval to follow the Vietcong (North Vietnamese troops) and eventually Prince Sihanouk gave his consent. Although desperate to remain independent, Prince Sihanouk knew that since the departure of the French the Cambodian economy was in real trouble, and was hoping for a generous injection of greenbacks. When American money failed to materialise, his thoughts turned north and he had plan to travel to the USSR and China seeking economic support and military aid against the Vietnamese. Ironically, Phnom Penh was drowning with American influences and culture. Young men grew their hair long, wore flared shirts and bell-bottom trousers and everyone listened to the westernized Cambodian music which was the latest fashion.

Behind the *joie de vivre*, however, Cambodia was being inexorably dragged into the Vietnam War. By March 1970, tensions were running high along the Cambodian-Vietnamese border and in Phnom Penh anti-Vietnamese sentiment was on the rise and outbreaks of racial hatred between Cambodian and Vietnamese were soon common. School teachers and student leaders organised anti-Vietnamese demonstrations which attacked both the North and South Vietnamese embassies in Phnom Penh demanding that the North Vietnamese Army leave Cambodia immediately. As a child, I heard chilling stories of torture being undertaken by both sides. The Vietnamese buried three Cambodians alive in a small triangle with only their heads above ground. A fire was lit in the middle and the Vietnamese boiled a kettle on it. The Cambodians would bind the hands of Vietnamese prisoners with wire punched through their palms before throwing them into the Mekong River to "swim home".

On March 18, 1970, Prince Sisowath Sirik Matak, Prince Sihanouk's cousin, and General Lon Nol, the self-proclaimed President of a newly created Khmer Republic, with the tacit support of the United States of America, staged a *coup d'Etat* to depose Prince Sihanouk while he was in Paris for medical treatment. The event marked the very fatal political turning point for the government and the people of Cambodia. It triggered a series of events that led to the greatest catastrophe and genocide in the history of Cambodia. It was an event that Prince Sisowath Sirik Matak, who was the main orchestrator, came to regret later and admitted in a letter to United States Ambassador to Cambodia, John Gunther Dean, that it was his biggest mistake in life.

A month after the coup, President Richard Nixon of the United States of America decided to invade Cambodia and begin carpet bombing along the Cambodian border in an effort to oust the Vietcong who had allegedly taken up position there. By August 1973[1] American B-52s had dropped more than two hundred thousand tons of bombs onto the region, equivalent to the amount of A-bomb dropped on Hiroshima in 1945. For the next five years, the war and bombing continued relentlessly

---

[1] While officially bombing of Cambodia by the USAF lasted from April 1970 until the American withdrawal from Vietnam in 1973, recent documents obtained from the White House under Freedom of Information legislation revealed the bombing had commenced as early as March 1969.

all around Cambodia's country side destroying the farmers and peasants' traditional way of life and tip the balance of power between the Royalist in the countryside and the Khmer Republican in the capital. Many Cambodian peasants and farmers were victims of the bombings. Lives were lost and a large proportion of those who survived saw their homes and livelihoods destroyed. Some fled the countryside to the capital, Phnom Penh, becoming refugees in their own country; and others took shelter in the jungle joining the revolution.

The relatively unknown Communist Party of Cambodia, Khmer Grahorm (literately translated as Red Khmer or better known as "Khmer Rouge"), was a group of revolutionists including students from Paris who had become its leaders. They began to wage a guerrilla war against the government and by the end of 1974 they had gained control of Siem Reap in the northwest as well as central region provinces such as Kampong Thom and upper Kampong Cham.

Anger with the American bombing, the coup and corruption contributed toward their popularity, particularly among peasants and farmers who they claimed to represent. Young peasants embraced their ideology. The Khmer Rouge ultimately came to power on April 17, 1975, a day when a cloud of darkness swept across Cambodia. The Khmer Rouge had the support of China, and like Prince Sihanouk, Pol Pot had also spent time there and was an enthusiastic admirer of Chairman Mao's "Great Leap Forward" although to what level he had read about the "Red Book" is unknown. One thing is apparent, however, and that is that he wanted to condense Mao's five-year plan into only four.

Under Pol Pot "Brother Number One", the Khmer Rouge turned Cambodian culture upside down and everything before April 17, 1975, must be deleted to build a new society. This was a revolution, named "agrarian socialism", against just about everything including capitalism, the residents of Phnom Penh and anything that could be considered bourgeois. The Khmer Rouge implemented a policy of genocide. So much pain, and suffering were inflicted upon the people of Cambodia and millions died under the regime.

Somehow, I survived, although I nearly didn't. After that, I, along with tens of thousands of my compatriots, became a refugee, and I lived through that experience as well, although it, too, was fraught with danger. I finally arrived in Australia in 1981. Since then I have tried to share my experiences with my friends and other interested Australians. Some laughed at my story, but others encouraged me to write it down. Over the years, I made many attempts to record my childhood experiences, my life in a labour camp, my separation from my family and my eventual escape across the border, but I was not able to continue beyond a few lines. Every time I sat down in front of a keyboard I would become very tired. Sadness would choke my words and tears would fill my eyes because my memories were just too painful.

Many people around the world finally learnt about the Cambodian genocide from "The Killing Fields". Like many survivors of this time I tried to move on with my life. It was easier to ignore my memories. Eventually I stopped trying to write. I locked my papers and letters away in a shoe box along with some old photos. It wasn't until 2014, with some time on my hands, when I was throwing away some unwanted books and folders that I came across the box again. I sat on the bed and gently took off the lid. The box held so much. Was it time to re-visit my past after all these years? Slowly I began to read.

As I flipped through the pages, I thought of an old friend of mine in London who had been asking me for my story for almost a decade, "When are you going to put your story together?" He had often pestered me over the years. "Writing down your memories will allow future generations to read and learn from history," he reminded me. His words resonated within me, *"future generations to read and learn"*. It is not my intention to write a book of Cambodia history or of the Cambodian genocide. There have been many stories and books written and successfully published, even films of Cambodian who survived the Khmer Rouge regime. I want this story to serve as a lesson for my own children, and perhaps their children too, to learn about their father's history. I remembered, too, that amongst the pain and grief, the sadness and horror of my ordeal, were many good things, too: courage, strength, power over evil, and hope.

This is my story.

Map of Cambodia

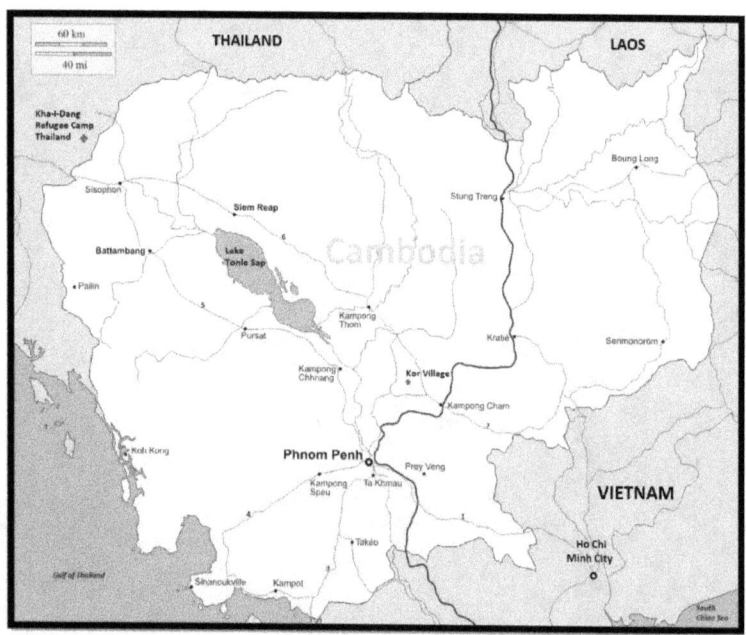

Two red dots on the map indicate Kor Village's proximity to Phnom Penh, and Khao-I-Dang Refugee Camp across the Cambodian borders.

Chapter One

Humble Beginnings

I was born and raised in a city that was once full of life - the city never sleeps. Phnom Penh was once the most beautiful city, a major capital and the jewel of Asia. My family was part of the ethnic minority making a living in the city but in those days, Chinese-Cambodian was the largest ethnic group in Phnom Penh. We had our own schools, Buddhist temples, Chinese-language newspapers, and even a hospital. Most of the shops, restaurants, and businesses were run by Chinese, so one could easily get by without speaking a single word of Khmer (Cambodian).

My mother didn't have the luxury of assuming the traditional role of a housewife when she married my father, she also ran a small shop at the market. I suppose Mama's strength and energy came from growing up in a very large family. In those days having as many as ten children was normal. There were nine in my mother's family. She was the third eldest, and had four brothers and four sisters. She was the slimmest and tallest of the girls, displaying a perfect mixture of her Khmer and Chinese heritage: an oval shaped face and olive skin, neither too fair nor too dark. Her nose was long like a Westerner.

Mama was second generation Cambodian-born Chinese and she grew up in a village called Kor in Kampong Cham province about a hundred kilometres from the city of Phnom Penh on the central lowlands of the Mekong River. In those days, many Chinese, especially those from Canton, came to find work or set up businesses in Cambodia. Because Kampong Cham was a port which serviced the merchants who came to buy rubber, timber, bananas and more, a large number of Chinese settled here. My great-grandfather was one of them, and once established he bought land and built a couple of large houses in the village. My grandfather on my mother's side inherited one of them.

Until she was married Mama never set foot outside of the village. Although a country girl, she learned other languages very quickly. She learnt to speak the Chinese dialect Teochew from helping her father run his business in the village, but her opportunities for formal education were limited. The schools in the area were few and far between and back then, too, most women stayed home to help with the housework.

My father was quite the opposite. He was born and raised in Phnom Penh and had never set foot on a farm. He also came from a big family. He had two younger brothers and four younger sisters, however, one of the girls, the family's second child, drowned in the river when she was only five. Despite a Khmer fortune teller warning her not to be cruel or take any life when she was pregnant his mother, my Grandma Lee, did her bit for the family and would assist the workers to cut up the fish, stabbing a knife into their heads and then gutting them while they flapped about, still alive. In Cambodia, we believe that there is life after death and that our spirit will live on for eternity. We believe that we will be reincarnated into a different life form, whether reborn as another human being or as an animal - life continues to recycle. When my father was born with an infection in his mouth, Grandma said it was a curse for her cruelty. The infection, like a boil, was very painful and my father was constantly crying. He couldn't drink milk and started to lose weight. Although the doctor had told her not to touch it, Grandma eventually took matters into her own hands and pricked it. While it relieved the pressure, it also damaged the roof of his mouth, so that he whistled when he breathed. When he began to speak, he sounded like someone with a cleft palate, meaning he was teased and given the nicknames.

In early 1960 my father travelled to China, looking for medical treatment for his speech impediment and wanting to further his Chinese education. (At that time, anyone with a parent born outside Cambodia was considered a foreigner, so Father was officially Chinese.) Unfortunately, he had no luck finding either a treatment or further learning in China, as he walked right into Chairman Mao's major economic and social reform plan, "The Great Leap Forward." It took him three years to make his way back home and to do that he had to stow away in the bottom of a cargo ship leaving Hong Kong. In the rush to depart he was forced to leave his documents behind, including his Chinese identification card.

Once back home Grandma Lee asked one of her relatives in Kor Village to bribe the village official so that Father ended up with a Khmer ID, and a new name: Chhorn. She also took this opportunity to find him a wife. Kor Village was a small community where everyone knew each other intimately. Father was summoned to Kor Village for the first time (although he would later spend far more time than he wanted there) to be inspected by eligible suitors. The matchmaker's husband was my mother's teacher at the school in the village and she felt like Father and Mama would be a good couple. This was quite normal in those days - marriage was all done via arrangement, and not by going on dates and falling in love. Both sets of parents agreed, and that's how they were married, despite the fact they didn't know each other at all.

Mama often joked and told us, "I only married your father because my parents made me. If it had been up to me, I would have chosen someone else. I was beautiful and had many admirers. Some even offered a pair of oxen as an engagement gift!"

My father had a sense of humour, so he could laugh along with us. He was good looking, although short and slim. Whenever they had their photo taken he would have Mama sit down so he could stand behind her, or he'd stand on tip toes so no one could tell he was shorter than her. He was the eldest son of the Lee family and a very proud man.

After they were married they moved to Phnom Penh. She had moved in with him, but also with his parents and four of his siblings. In Chinese tradition, the daughter-in-law of the eldest son must take care of his family. This was the opposite of Khmer tradition where the son would move out with his new wife, while the daughter would bring her husband to live with her and take care of her family.

"Living with your grandparents was not rent free!" my mother often complained. "I had to pay half the rent from the little income that I earned from reselling raisins. *And* do all the housework."

Grandma enjoyed telling Mama of all the servants they once had, and how her father's fishing business had been the largest in Phnom Penh. It was so successful that her father was eventually given the ultimate authority by the king, the power to "kill first and talk later." Unfortunately, this fortune had been lost by my grandmother's eldest brother after my great grandfather died.

After about six months Mama could stand it no longer. The domestic duties, the responsibilities of the household and the lack of money all contributed to her frustration and feeling that she was a slave. She gave my father an ultimatum, either they moved out together or Mama would move out on her own. Papa had no choice. My grandmother was unimpressed, but Mama let her know how she felt.

"I do housework all day. There is very little money coming in, and much more money going out! I am spending all of the wedding gift money my mother gave me!"

At that time, Phnom Penh was a true melting pot with many different ethnic groups living together in harmony. The ethnic Vietnamese and the Muslim Cambodians would be busy fishing. The Khmer farmer's wives dominated the marketplaces with fruits, vegetables and poultry from their farms. The Chinese ran shops, cafes and restaurants. We all went about our daily lives and minded our own business. Everyone was friendly and polite and the neighbours all knew each other's names. We did not shake hands or hug when we met like Americans did, however, but greeted each other in the Khmer manner by putting our palms together, pressing them against our chest, just beneath the chin and bowing slowly forward. This was our sign of respect for each other.

Mama became pregnant with me and she and Father eventually moved out to share a house with my father's cousin in Pochentong Market, near the airport. It was also close to a school and Mama quickly identified a business opportunity and started selling shaved ice topped with red beans and Nestlé condensed milk, as well as candies, notebooks, chalks and pencils to the local kids.

A few months later, during the Water Festival in mid-November I was brought into this world. Grandfather Lee named me "Lee Huy" but all my relatives called me "Ah-Lak". Ah-Lak, meant bald head, which was my nickname when I was born nearly hairless. My birth might have been a joyful gift to the Lee family, but we were not rich like my grandmother's family had been. Grandma had wanted my mother to deliver me at one of the best hospitals in Phnom Penh but Mama had not realised what the city midwife would charge - back in her village a midwife would be happy if she was offered a couple of sarongs or a few kilos of rice. Here in Phnom Penh, she was now faced with a medical bill of 2000 riels!

Her market stall took in less than one hundred riels per day, however, half of that went on costs. 2000 riels was a lot to pay. When she ran out of her wedding present money and had no more gold jewellery to pawn, she had to borrow from our friends and neighbours. This was a common form of lending in Cambodia, because borrowing money from banks just wasn't an option in those days. Instead, local people, who knew and trusted each other, each put in a small amount of money into a pot every month. If a syndicate member wanted to buy something large, borrowing from the money in the pot was an option.

Mama lacked a formal education but was street smart and very good with people. Despite struggling for several years with her business and taking care of her family, she always remained optimistic. She believed that education and knowledge were the best survival tools. Her only regret was that she did not have the opportunity to acquire either herself. She was determined to make sure that I, her children to come and even her younger siblings all received a proper schooling.

Mama probably would have managed better back in the

village, in the environment she was familiar with, but now she did the best she could with the limited resources available. She decided to move the family across to the east of the city where rent was cheaper. We moved to a working class Chinese district called Kandal Market, literally, the market in the middle. It was about a kilometre in each direction to the Independence Monument in the southeast of the city and Wat Phnom, a popular Khmer Buddhist temple on top of a small hill in its heart. Our new home was only a few minutes' walk away from the Royal Palace and just a few blocks away from the Sisowath quay where the Mekong River joined the Tonle Sap River. The locals called this intersection the River of Four Faces, as you could travel in four directions from this point: up the Tonle Sap to the famous Lake Tonle Sap, up the Mekong all the way to the Himalayan foothills, down the Mekong to Vietnam or down the Bassac River, which branches off the Mekong River and runs parallel to it.

For me the move was great as I now had easy access to a whole world of palaces and temples and the excitement of the quay. For Mama, it offered an abundance of business opportunities. Goods from Vietnam and China arrived on the docks and there were cargo loading companies, warehouses and shops all along the river front. Because of Prince Sihanouk's strong ties with China, a lot of Chinese merchants were setting up businesses in Phnom Penh. Prince Sihanouk even named one of the main streets in Phnom Penh after Chairman Mao as a sign of his friendship: Mao Tse Tong Boulevard. While Cambodia received some financial support from China, many believed this was only so Cambodia would support Mao's efforts to have the Chinese communist party recognised at the UN as the legitimate government of China rather than the Kuomintang Nationalists, still the main political party of Taiwan.

Our new place in Kandal Market was only small, a four-by-four metre unit with brick walls, a concrete floor and a little wooden loft about two metres above the ground. The entire floor space was smaller than a modern double bedroom. It was an old warehouse converted into one-room apartments for those who could not afford a proper house. There was no yard and every apartment had a single wooden front door and one window with two wooden panes and iron bars. We had to share toilet facilities with the other residents. The whole complex was not even on the street - it was sandwiched between three buildings in a narrow, concrete alley that was wet all the time. There were no sinks, showers or baths, so all washing: of people, eating utensils and clothes alike, took place in a large cement jar at the front door. Water came from the roof in the wet season or from a nearby tap when it was dry. Apart from the night time when everyone had gone to bed, there would always be some residents either doing their washing, cooking or having their meal in the alley. The alley was our large living room. Behind the block was a Pepsi Cola factory where they made ice and soft drinks. Across the alley was a two-storey block of terraces. These had shops at ground level and flats above. Access to our house was either via the damp lane or through a tunnel under a five-storey building to the north.

Mama was soon working hard and using her canny business experience to sell everything she could find: from imported Chinese canned foods, sardines in tomato sauce, sugar, cooking oil, Nestlé condensed milk from Switzerland and powdered-baby milk from France. She bought her stock directly from the ships which docked along the riverbank. She was soon so busy running both her business and her family that she brought one of her younger sisters, my Aunt Hiam, to help. Hiam was twelve, and as well as looking after me, Mama made sure she also attended school.

Mama's business kept growing and was soon making enough that she had to rent the apartment next door to keep her stock in - and there was room in it for a bed of my own! No longer did I have to share with my parents. No more sleeping near their feet and falling out in the middle of the night! Over the next three years my brothers Huang and Chong were born, and they now shared Mama and Father's bed while I, Aunt Hiam, and Uncle Yu (sixth of the family who had moved in with us to attend university) had the new room in the second apartment. Mama had a good head-start and well established relationships with her regular customers and suppliers, and they all trusted her. Every morning she'd be up early, heading straight to the docks looking for new merchandise to buy while Yu and Hiam set up her stall in the market. Things were going well for a while.

CHAPTER TWO

IT ENDED EVEN BEFORE IT BEGAN

Due to my Chinese heritage, I had been sent to the local Chinese primary school, rather than attending a standard Khmer school. I remember the first day: I was dressed in a white short sleeved shirt, a pair of navy shorts and a shiny new pair of shoes. (I had no way of knowing that it would be another fifteen years until I would put on another pair of new shoes.) I also had my very first bag, one that had a strap to go over my shoulder. Inside it were a couple of notebooks and a pencil case with a few sharpened pencils. That first day I was excited even before I left the house. When my mother dropped me at the school, however, suddenly I was terrified by the unfamiliar faces. I watched my Mama start to leave. As she walked towards the gate I started to cry. The snivel turned into a piteous howl and before long, I started to kick the ground. When she ignored my tantrum, I ran across the playground towards her, still stamping my feet, hoping to get her to change her mind. I had wanted to stay at school but also did not want Mama to leave me. A tug of-war went on for a several minutes until a teacher came and finally dragged me into the classroom.

As my sobbing eventually subsided I realised I had found an admirer. She was a girl of my age with soft, fair skin, and dark hair cut short to just above her shoulders. She had beautiful almond-shaped eyes, like all Chinese eyes, but her nose was slightly flatter than mine. When she smiled, she had one front tooth missing just like me. Her name was *Pei Ai* (full of love). She sat next to me and tried to comfort me. We quickly became best friends. Back at home, my aunts and uncles would tease me by saying, "Hey, how's your new love, Pei Ai, your new girlfriend, has she given you a kiss yet?"

What did I know about love at that age? I blushed and my face went bright scarlet every time they teased me. Sadly, my puppy love romance ended even before it began and my time with Pei Ai was too short lived as I wasn't to spend very long at the school.

In March that year, racial tension had escalated and anti-Vietnamese sentiment was at a boiling point. Demonstrations were organised by university students and supporters of Lon Nol to attack the Vietnamese embassies. There were frequent rallies and protests in the park behind the market. Uncle Yu was amongst them demanding the Vietnamese to get out of Cambodia. There were loud speakers, chanting and music. There was even a circus of motorbike riders attempting to ride their bikes up the wall of the park. It just seemed like one long party to me. In my spare time, I often climbed up a tree to have a good look at it, although I didn't understand what it was about. A week later General Lon Nol, the Prime Minister, along with Prince Sihanouk's cousin, Prince Sisowath Sirik Matak, helped by the United States of America, staged a *coup d'Etat* to depose the Prince Sihanouk government. Prince Sihanouk was away in Paris having medical treatment when General Lon Nol appointed himself as the President of Cambodia Republic on March 18, 1970.

Prince Sihanouk then turned to China for support and took shelter in Peking (now known as Beijing). Because of Prince Sihanouk's involvement with China and the incursions into Cambodia by the North Vietnamese, also supported by China, strong anti-Chinese sentiment began to grow. Not long after, studying Chinese became prohibited. Chinese schools and newspapers were closed and were replaced with English ones. My Chinese education was cut short after six months - and this meant there was no more school for the rest of the year.

With school closed, I spent most of my time at home training my pet Siamese fighting fish (*Trey Krem* in Khmer). Fighting fish come in many colours, but generally bright red or vivid purple-blue, or a mix of both. The males have large, flowing fins and are very aggressive. When two are put into the same tank they fight to the death. Mine was in a glass jar filled two thirds full, and I hid it in a dark corner of the house. I trained him by using a mirror. As soon he saw his reflection he'd flare his gills, expand his fins, curve his body and sway from side to side and hit his head against the wall of his tank. He'd press his body against the glass and flip his tail, getting ready to fight. He didn't realise he was looking at himself. I kept him in the dark so he would be more aggressive.

A fight would last up to ten minutes. We'd put the fish in the same container and then place it on a bench. All the boys would gather round, as one of the owners I had the best seat, right next to the jar. At first the fish would show off, arcing their bodies and flipping their tails against each other. They'd expand their gills, making them look larger to intimidate the opponent. They'd swim around in figure eights until suddenly the fight began. They'd jab and bite, tearing off fins and scales until one was exhausted. Occasionally, their mouths would be locked together and they'd frantically twist and gyrate until they were able to separate. By the end of the fight their fins looked like old seaweed. My fish was a good fighter, I'd always let his fins heal before letting him fight his next bout. He won his matches until one day when Small Uncle (he was known as Small not because of his size but because he was my father's youngest brother) brought his fish to fight mine. Small Uncle was already twenty but single, and his only job was to help Grandma Lee set up her fabric shop in the morning and pack it up in the evening. I agreed to the match, and as usual there were some bets placed as kids attempted to increase their pocket money. Small Uncle's fish was young and lacked experience, and the match was over in a couple of minutes. Then Small Uncle lost his temper, reached in and grabbed my fish and slammed it onto the floor. I was distraught, and cried loudly.

Small Uncle offered to buy me a new fish, but I didn't want a new one, I missed my old one! He was a bad loser and later he did the same thing to my cricket. In Cambodia, we not only ate insects, we sometimes kept them as pets. We kept field crickets in matchboxes and like the fish, would set them up to fight each other. When my cricket beat Small Uncle's, he pulled its head off. I ran over to Grandma's shop in tears, despites his threats that he would hit me if I told her. I didn't care, I was tired of my pets being killed! Grandma couldn't believe that a grown man was playing with children. Her solution was to find him a wife. Small Uncle settled down with a woman called Keang, although this wasn't to be the only time he was mean to me - despite the fact that my quick actions were one day to save him from a lot of pain and misery.

The only other school near us was the Wat Ounalom Buddhist temple where the pupils were taught Khmer and Cambodian Buddhist script. However, to be accepted into this school I had to become an apprentice and serve as a junior monk in the monastery until graduation!

Grandfather Lee was very much against the idea of sending me to a Khmer school believing that I should only attend a Chinese one. Even after all the years he had lived in Phnom Penh he still refused to speak Khmer. He called the beautiful curly symbolic Cambodian script "crab writing," as if a crab had been dipped in black ink and been left to wiggle on a piece of paper making marks that no one could read or understand.

As I was not attending school Grandfather Lee used to pick me up for his regular Chinese breakfast before he headed off to work as an accountant at a Chinese merchant shop. We would sit on round stools at a stainless-steel table, always in the same corner of the same Chinese café. I remember hearing the waiters shouting into the kitchen whenever they took an order. My grandfather had been coming here so often, always ordering the same thing that he no longer spoke to them. They would automatically bring his long black coffee with no sugar and a plate of deep fried Chinese cakes. He would order a glass of hot soybean milk with a couple of raw eggs whipped into the milk for me. Soy milk was cheap in Phnom Penh. My mother told me that the reason I had smooth milky skin and a fair complexion was because she used to drink soy milk every morning when she was pregnant. I loved my mornings with my grandfather. He was a man of very few words. He was just like an ancient Chinese philosopher, of average height and skinny like a stick, very gentle and mellow. He never raised his voice even when he was angry. He would sit there silently waiting for his coffee to come in a French Duralex glass. Grandfather Lee would pick up the rim at the top of the hot glass between his thumb and index finger, turn it 180 degrees and begin to slowly sip. In between each savoured mouthful, he took a puff of smoke from the cigarette in his left hand. By the stains on his teeth that I knew he had been performing this ritual since long before I was born. Sometimes he would break into speech, lectures for me on Chinese philosophy, ones that he had made up for himself which I never understood.

Sadly though, these are my last memories of grandfather on my father's side, as the war was soon to arrive and change everything.

Chapter Three

Father Missed His Plane

In early 1971 some of my old Chinese teachers opened a new school, opposite the park, and not far from my mother's stall. They told Mama it was a "Khmer English" school and asked if she would be interested enrolling me there. It was true that they taught some English - but they also taught Mandarin and maths. I can't remember learning any Khmer there. The pupils were all Chinese; most of them did not speak Khmer. Perhaps, like Grandfather Lee, their parents prohibited them from speaking Khmer or even playing with Khmer kids. The woman whom Small Uncle just married, Keang, could hardly speak Khmer. She had very limited vocabularies and spoke with a very strong Chinese accent. Mama and I often giggled and made fun of her accent. The other market stall parents would ask Mama why she sent me to such an expensive school to study English.

"*Mae Ah-Di*, (Mother of the little boy) why did you enrol *Ah-Di* (the boy) in an English school?"

"I can't let him play around at home doing nothing all day," Mama replied proudly.

She felt English was going to be an important language for me to know. She was right, although she couldn't have had any idea just how vital it would be. Back then, English was not spoken by many Cambodians. French was the second official language and it was taught to senior students. It was sometimes even used in news bulletins. Occasionally we heard Prince Sihanouk speaking it, although to me his squeaky voice just sounded like he was angry. I had no idea what he was saying, although every now and again I heard the words "Amerika" and "Khmer Rouge". I paid no attention. I just wished that it would end quickly so the music would come back on.

We had no TV at home so our only entertainment was the radio. I loved listening to Khmer songs and stories narrated over the radio with my Aunt Hiam. As the year went on, more schools starting teaching English and I heard less of Prince Sihanouk's squeaky voice on the radio. Soon Khmer songs started being replaced with English and American ones. I was even made to practice an American song at school when one of the teachers brought his guitar in and taught us "Beautiful Sunday." We repeated after the teacher.

Sunday morning up with the lark
I think I'll take a walk in the park
Hey hey hey, it's a beautiful day

It wasn't long before even the traditional Cambodian temple schools started night classes in English. As a result, a year after starting at my private "English" school, I was also enrolled in English lessons at the Wat Ounalom Buddhist temple near my house. These classes were free and designed for young people who had to work or to attend Cambodian schools during the day. Students in their late teens were very surprised to see me, a little seven-year-old boy, in the same classroom as them. I was proud to be the youngest, and sitting in the same room as Aunt Heng, my father's youngest sister, studying "Essential English for Foreign Students" Book II by C. E. Eckersley. (I had already completed Book 1 at school).

The first time Aunt Heng saw me, she told me I was in the wrong class because she was embarrassed in case her classmates found out that I was her nephew. She would sit on the other side of the room. I knew why she was embarrassed, because I usually sat right near the front, very comfortable in a large chair, its right arm expanding into a writing desk - which was just big enough for me to rest my head on and go to sleep.

One night the monk who was teaching us had pairs of students read dialogue from the textbook to each other. When it came to my turn, however I didn't know where to start because I had been asleep. After this he would skip past me and let me stay sleeping. I acquired a nickname when the teacher and his students started calling me Bob, after a character in the textbook who also kept falling asleep in class.

Being a teenager in Cambodia in the early seventies generally meant you were having a good time. American influence and hippie culture were everywhere. Men grew their hair to their shoulders and blow waved it. They wore bright shirts and bell-bottom trousers. The bigger the bell bottoms, the more fashionable they were. Uncle Yu was one of them, and was famous for asking his tailor to make his trouser bottoms wide enough to cover his toes. He came home one day to show off.

"They're too big!" I said. The bottom of each leg could have fitted my whole body inside it.

"Little boy, what do you know?" Uncle Yu retaliated.

Listening to westernized Cambodian music also became popular. An Italian brand of scooter, the Vespa, also started to make an appearance. Women in particular, liked it because it had fully enclosed bodywork that went all the way up to form a tall splash guard at the front. As Cambodian women are taught to sit with their legs together from a young age, the design of the Vespa was perfect for them as they could rest their feet behind the splash guard without having to spread their legs like a conventional motorbike. Couples would ride around on them with him driving and her sitting side saddle behind. Vespas were soon in every corner of the city. Mama even bought one as a delivery vehicle.

Like the Vespa, Mama's business was also flourishing. She had made enough money to buy some electrical appliances for us, including a very expensive electronic rice cooker. We no longer needed to light a fire to cook rice, which was good news for Aunty Hiam, a well-known rice pot burner.

What I loved the most was a new toy of my father's: an eight-track player. A forerunner of cassettes, it had a magnetic tape which passed around a few spinning wheels to another large reel. The annoying feature was that the whole twenty-centimetre cartridge contained just one song and had to be rewound if you wanted to hear it again. I was forbidden from touching it though: only Papa had that right. Like the Lee household, for us it seemed like the whole of Cambodia was booming. It was a time of joy and prosperity. It was a time of plenty.

Away from the good times in the city, however, the countryside was at war. American B52s continuously bombed the regions along the border with Vietnam in an effort to oust the Vietcong who were still entering Cambodia. Peasants and farmers became victims. Many of those who survived lost their homes and their livelihoods. They fled to the city, refugees in their own country. I began to see homeless people begging for handouts in the streets around the market. Khmer country kids roamed from one Chinese restaurant to another looking for leftover food on the tables. The waiters would yell out in Chinese, "Get out, get out of here!" and would then mutter "Khmer kids" in a tone that implied they were an inferior race.

In the north west of Cambodia lay Angkor Wat, an ancient temple lying among the trees - but it was not the only thing in this jungle. The Khmer Rouge was forming itself in an effective guerrilla army. Many of its founders, such as Brother Number 1, Pol Pot, Brother Number 3 Ieng Sery, Brother Number 4 Khieu Samphan and Son Sen the sixth brother were the same middle class intellectuals who had come under the thrall of Marxism and Mao while studying in France. Their numbers had grown dramatically with the influx of peasants and farmer's sons and daughters, angry at both the continual B52 bombing raids and the poverty they were now enduring having been forced away from their lands. Opposition to Prince Sihanouk had forced the Khmer Rouge into the jungle, ironically because of the levels of corruption demonstrated by Lon Nol government, the coup that dethroned him brought even more recruits to the cause.

Another source of frustration came from the refugees in Phnom Penh noticing that the city dwellers were relatively unaffected by the war and seemed to have plenty to eat. They began to believe the Khmer Rouge's propaganda that the city residents were exploiting the system. There was a saying in Cambodia at that time, "Trees grow on farms but their fruits ripen in the city." The younger refugees had seen their parents working tirelessly to grow food, now they saw it ending up on the plates of the city dwellers, while they themselves remained without. They believed in the propaganda that the city dwellers had been stealing the fruits from their trees and all the produce of their hard labour for all these years.

Prince Sihanouk's squeaky voice on the radio from Peking claimed to be everything: The Prime Minister, the Prince, the King Father and any other symbol of power for the people of Cambodia. He was desperate, but he'd chosen the wrong ally in China, because he was pinning his hopes to *their* ally, the Khmer Rouge. He saw the Khmer Rouge as an instrument of his return to Phnom Penh and his broadcasts on Peking Radio called for rebellion against America, against the American backed Lon Nol government. Even after four years of absence, Prince Sihanouk was still enormously popular, especially amongst peasants and farmers, although he was less liked by the ethnic Chinese merchants and businessmen in Phnom Penh. He was a useful symbol for the Khmer Rouge, who used the call of "The return of King Father!" to rally Khmer peasants and farmers to the cause. Having the support of Prince Sihanouk meant the Chinese offered the Khmer Rouge weapons and training. More and more young peasants joined up, and from a handful of jungle fighters they developed into a well-armed force of more than two hundred thousand soldiers.

Grandma had a different nickname for Prince Sihanouk every time she heard him. He was Fat Boy, the Short Guy, even Playboy because of the affairs he'd had before his marriage. (His eldest daughter was from a liaison with one of the royal dancers.)

Because of the Prince Sihanouk's relationship with China the Cambodian government continued to manipulate the Khmers against the Chinese. We were an easy target. As well as our schools and newspapers (which had already been closed down) many Chinese shops and restaurants were also forced to close and because of the war and issues with supply, food prices were rising rapidly. Some shops were forced to increase their prices daily. In 1974 as rice, meat, chicken and vegetable prices soared, the blame was put on the Chinese. We also became a target for Lon Nol's Military Police who would come into shops and take whatever they wanted. Some businesses were forced to close after they were looted. The Military Police came to the market looking for their daily "tax collection." If we refused to pay, they would confiscate our goods and destroy our stalls. My mother would give them cans of sardines in tomato sauce or Nestlé condensed milk in lieu of payment.

Meanwhile the government was turning a blind eye to the crime and corruption now rampant in Phnom Penh. The rich could get away with murder by bribing police or the judiciary, and the poor were losing everything, including their opportunity for education. Students from poor families could not pass their exams if they could not afford a bribe for the teacher. For the rich, however, simply having a connection with a Lon Nol official would earn them the privilege of "friends with benefits." Inevitably some even turned their attention to the small stallholders, like Mama, wrongly accusing them of petty theft in order to extort payment for their release from jail, splitting their profits with generals and judges.

One afternoon I heard loud voices outside our house. Mama came rushing in followed by two men from the neighbourhood and a police officer. Some neighbours and their kids gathered near the door to find out what was going on. "Pa-Ah-Di and Ah-Hiam," Mama called to Father and Aunt Hiam, "I need you to look after the stall while I go to the police station." She sounded nervous.

It turned out that two men from the neighbourhood, who were brothers, were accusing Mama of stealing several ounces of their gold. One of them, named Jing, had some connection to a three-stripe general. The first thing Mama had known about the accusation was when the military police and the brothers had arrived at her stall demanding she accompany them to the police station in their jeep.

"Yes, *Meng* (Aunt) get into the jeep now," echoed Jing and

his brother.

The police officer's eyes flitted from Mama to the brothers then back to my mother.

"For what reason?" asked Mama.

"We'll talk when we get to the police station," replied the policeman.

"Yes, you'll find out at the police station," the two brothers said.

The policeman looked a bit irritated, but before he could say anything my mother made a request.

"Alright then, but I want to go home to tell my husband first."

"There's no need for that," replied the policeman.

"I have to let my family know where I am and organise someone to look after the stall," Mama explained.

Once he realised what was going on, my father was speechless. He didn't say anything as he left for the market. Once at the police station Mama learned from the brothers what she was accused of.

"You must tell the truth about the gold," the police officer told her.

"The truth about what gold?" Mama asked them.

"Where is it?" the policeman asked.

"I don't know anything about any gold," Mama replied.

"*Meng* must tell the truth," the policeman insisted.

"I didn't take their gold, so how can I confess and plead guilty to stealing it?" Mama told him again.

"If she doesn't admit to it, tie her up and pour fish sauce into her mouth!" Jing added from the side line.

My mother took one look at Jing and turned back to the policeman, "Pour fish sauce into my mouth, is that the right thing to do?"

"Let's take her to a higher level for judgement," Jing insisted.

The policeman lost his temper. "Are you in charge here, or am I?!" he shouted at Jing.

Their argument had become so loud that it could be heard

by a general next door. He ordered them all into his office. As they entered he was given a salute by the policeman. Mama greeted him in the respectful Khmer manner, putting her palms together, touching them to her chest and bowing. The general appeared to appreciate this, and he began asking her questions. She replied truthfully, always referring to him as *Lok* (sir). She explained how Jing and his brother were racketeers, known to falsely accuse people in the Kandal Market so they could extort money from them. To his credit, the general began to smell a large, dead rat. He had Jing's brother's servant brought in, as she was allegedly the main witness. He ordered everyone out and questioned the servant alone in his office. A short time later the door swung open, and the servant was snivelling. She had been told to lie to the police, or else be fired. She was only fourteen and her parents relied on her income to support their family back in her village. Mama was very lucky to have come across an honest general, as she explained to us when she finally returned home late that evening. The next morning the young girl came to apologise and say goodbye to Mama. The general had ordered Jing's brother to pay her a good sum of money as a penalty. She had the opportunity to return home or find work elsewhere. We all knew that Mama had had a lucky escape. The corruption was so widespread that most people didn't stand a chance of getting a fair trial.

 The Khmer Rouge were drawing ever closer; cutting off the highways and main avenues to Phnom Penh and the city's food and goods supplies. Thus, inflation was out of control. A kilo of pork now cost a sack of riels. The largest denomination had been the 100 riel note, but it was no longer sufficient. The government introduced a 500 riel note and was considering a 1000 riel note as well. By 1974 cash was nearly worthless. It became very difficult for Mama to obtain goods from the importers and she had to use gold to pay for her goods. When I was born, the midwife's demand for 2000 riels was equivalent to just over an ounce of gold, but after Lon Nol's coup the price rose to 3500. Towards the end of the Lon Nol government, it had risen to a staggering 400,000 per ounce.

Despite the price of a one-way plane ticket out of Phnom Penh increasing to more than a million riels (or over USD29,000), the rich residents of Phnom Penh and Chinese people with family or friends outside Cambodia were leaving the country like rats fleeing a sinking ship. Most of those who were lucky enough to get a ticket out, some of whom had to also pay for a fake passport, had already left by the end of 1974. I often heard Mama saying how this family had gone or that relative had left. Even the Vietnamese were fleeing South East Asia via Cambodia by bribing officials in the Cambodian immigration department and buying fake passports. The price of plane tickets went up daily as demand grew and fewer planes landed at Pochentong International Airport. Grandma Lee's elder brother and his two children had already gone to Thailand, from there they went on to America. Mama wanted to leave as well, but we didn't have enough money for one ticket, let alone the whole family. Unless, there was miracle or we would be stuck here with the rest of the residents who could not afford a plane ticket. Eventually the airport and a few other important facilities such as the oil refinery were bombed by the Khmer Rouge and, with Phnom Penh surrounded, the airport was closed. The last planes I saw were the square twin-tailed ones which flew low over Phnom Penh dropping propaganda leaflets. Every time this happened, I would have fun catching the leaflets before they hit the ground, but I had absolutely no idea what they said. On one of the leaflets, there was a cartoon picture of a Khmer man holding on to a rope between a tree branch hanging over the river where a crocodile in the river was waiting with its mouth wide open and a tiger walking on the tree branch. The caption read, "In the water there are crocodiles, up above there are tigers."

The Khmer Rouge was steadily advancing on Phnom Penh, and we now started hearing the sounds of machine guns and rocket fire in the distance. Shells began to be fired into the city. I soon learned to distinguish the different sounds of an approaching rocket. A hissing *weeeee* meant it had further to go, but a *crack-crack-crack* meant run for shelter immediately. Every time I heard this sound I would hide under the table of Mama's market stall. I was taught to stay flat on the ground, being told that if the rocket didn't land on me directly, its shrapnel could still take off my legs, or hit me in the stomach so I died a long, painful death. Despite my fear, Mama and the neighbours laughed every time they saw me on the ground my head inside a cardboard box tilted to one side with my bottom stuck high up in the air.

The rockets were coming from all directions, fired by the Khmer Rouge guerrillas on the other side of both the Mekong and Tonle Sap rivers. Possibly they were aiming at something strategic, but many dropped onto markets and schools, scattering shrapnel in all directions. Many innocent people were killed and injured. One bomb exploded close to the market near my old Chinese school. I saw kids being carried away with blood dripping from their wounded bodies as they were rushed to hospital on cyclo-rickshaws. One afternoon I was with my father fixing my little bicycle when we heard the rattling sound of a rocket approaching. It was going to fall somewhere near us. The sound was so close we realised we had no time to run. Father and I dropped flat on our faces. Then: *crack-crack-crack* and *bang!* We were shaken and our house was shaken. The rocket had hit the wall of the Pepsi Cola building just behind our apartment. If the building had been just a few metres lower it would have landed right on our house. The explosion was so loud my ears were ringing. We all ran outside to take a closer look at the damage. The wall must have been strong, as there was nothing major to see, and both Father and I were grateful for the solid concrete that had been used to make it.

Lessons at my new school were frequently interrupted for a week or two at a time as there were concerns we could be targeted. Then one day the school was closed and lessons were suspended indefinitely as the Khmer Rouge launched their final full scale assault on Phnom Penh.

With no idea of what was to come, I spent most of the time hanging around the market or playing with other kids near the Pepsi Cola building. Unconcerned about the war and unaware of the danger, we, children, soon found a new toy to play with: gun powder. Both the charcoal-like gun powder from AK47 bullets as well as the clear yellowish plastic explosive from unexploded bombs were now readily available to us. We removed the projectile and emptied the gunpowder from the AK47 bullet case. We then wedged the case between two hard bricks and hammered the primer with a nail to make it explode loudly. We'd spread gun powder onto the silver-coated paper from the inside of a cigarette packet and roll both ends of the paper tight. We then lit one end of the paper and stood back to watch the gunpowder flare, the case spinning out of control, sparkling like fireworks and emitting huge amounts of thick, white smoke. The smell was sensational. It didn't occur to us that we were now playing with explosives and bullets where only recently we had been having games of marbles, throwing bottle caps, tossing coins into holes and flicking rubber bands.

It was all fun until one morning. I had just woken up, playing with a mate of mine and Lily, my little white Pekinese dog and her puppies. Suddenly some kids from the alley outside rushed into our apartment, shouting. "It's him. It's that Chinese boy!" Apparently, a neighbour's boy, whom I often played with, had had his trouser pockets full of gunpowder. One of his rolled gunpowder fireworks had spun out of control, and a spark had ignited his stash, and now half his body had been badly burned. The kid's father was a soldier for Lon Nol and I was being accused of being complicit in the accident. I was lucky that I had my friend there as a witness to my non-involvement, otherwise I might have been in deeper trouble than Mama had had with Jing.

The bombing and shooting intensified, worse at night, and lasted for weeks. Rockets and artillery fire rained down on Phnom Penh every evening, and the sky was full of bright flashes as they exploded. When the warning siren went off we would gather our mattresses and blankets to find what protection we could underneath the tall concrete archway which was the entrance to our alley. Bombs were landing around the city indiscriminately and more than a hundred of us, young and old alike, were crammed into the thirty square metres of the tiny alley, praying that the walls would be strong enough to protect us. The old grandmothers sat in a circle every night, their legs folded to the right, with their hands together, praying for us all to be safe. They said, *"Na Mo Ta Sha, Ha Ra Wat Tao,"* a traditional Khmer Buddhist prayer but their prayer was often interrupted by the sound of the blasting bomb in the distance. I would sometimes fall asleep to the sweet rhythm of their humming. As the government had imposed a curfew, even on the rare nights there was no warning siren we still had nothing to do from eight o'clock in the evening. As the Khmer Rouge grew closer the curfew was extended to twenty-four hours. The streets were empty, even though it was the Khmer Lunar New Year, when normally they would be packed. Usually at this time I would visit the monks with Mama, and play traditional games with Aunt Hiam. We would have music around a fire, and dance the *Rormvong* at Wat Phnom temple. I was considered a good *Rormvong* dancer. This year there was nothing.

My father, who drove a white Mercedes taxi for a living, was one of the few people who were busy. He was transporting Americans from their embassy to helicopters landing in the middle of a school ground. When he came home after work, he said, *"Ah-Barang* (the French) and *Ah-meric* (the Americans) all flew away." On his last trip, he was ordered to transport Prince Sihanouk's eldest daughter, Princess Buppha Devi, to a helicopter. She was not well and had to be helped to get out of my father's car by one of her royal housemaids. Father said that as he waited by the helicopter an American GI had asked if he wanted to go with them. He said no, of course, not wanting to leave us, his wife and children, behind. If he had known the opportunity existed he would have had us all waiting near the helicopters, ready to fly to America. How different our lives would have been?

We knew with the Americans gone it wouldn't be long. Barely any shops were open. We sat at home, waiting and wondering what would happen.

It was now in mid-April, we reached the eve of the end of the war, although we did not recognise it for that immediately. We hoped the Khmer Luna New Year would bring us peace, but we had no idea what the peace would bring with it.

CHAPTER FOUR

THE LONG MARCH

Dawn of April 17, 1975, and everything was disturbingly quiet. There were no sirens, no machine guns, and no bombs exploding. The sun came up for air after a good night's sleep and hung languidly above the horizon. Golden rays reflected off the slow, muddy Mekong River. It had been a long time since I had been able to sleep through the whole night without being disturbed. Although we had gone to bed in the alley, I must have been carried back inside our house during the night. I woke up to a very hot April's breeze. It was the beginning of spring in the northern hemisphere, but it was the end of our dry season here. The smell of the approaching monsoon season was all around us, but this year the monsoon was not alone. It had company, and although we could not see it, a cloud of darkness was sweeping across Cambodia.

The Khmer Rouge triumphantly seized control of the capital. Although we had feared a protracted siege with all the destruction that would come with it, in the end they just marched into Phnom Penh without opposition because Lon Nol's army had fled. White flags were everywhere. The Khmer Rouge drove their tanks and trucks filled with young soldiers through the main streets. The soldiers wore black uniforms which looked like pyjamas and a plain Chinese communist cap (without the red star). They also wore a red checkered *Krama* - the traditional Cambodian scarf which had become their trademark - wrapped around either their necks or heads. Some of them were only a few years older than me, perhaps twelve or thirteen. They all carried machine guns and grenade launchers. (I thought the rockets in the ends of the bazookas looked like banana flowers.) They showed very little emotion.

Many of the Kandal Market residents thought nothing was wrong. They were happy the fighting was over and went out to cheer the great victory. They wanted to thank the Khmer

Rouge for liberating Cambodia from American imperialism. They were looking forward to the return of the King Father. In those first few hours of that warm April morning many Cambodians rejoiced that the war was over.

Unknown to us, the Khmer Rouge had a different agenda and their revolution was never meant to simply liberate Cambodia from Lon Nol and the Americans. They had no intention of bringing peace and prosperity. Their young and innocent faces were the faces of peasants and farmers with limited or no education. They had been brainwashed by their leaders. They were too young to realise what was happening or to understand the concepts of revolution and communist ideology. They were barely old enough to be concerned about death. The only difference between them and me was that they carried guns and grenades while I ran every time I heard the sound of a bomb exploding.

After I finished my typical Chinese family breakfast of rice porridge, white radish pickles, roasted peanuts and salted duck eggs, I went for a walk. There was something taking place on the main road, Preah Norodom Boulevard, only a couple of blocks away. Mama had already gone on her bicycle to find out what was going on in the rest of the city.

As I walked along the streets with Lily I felt excitement and relief everywhere. "Peace. Peace. The war is over!" Many people cheered in French, some saying they had heard already that the King Father had returned to Cambodia[2].

Before I had gone too far, however, I was intercepted by Mama and she ordered me back home immediately. From her expression, I could tell something was wrong. She looked as if she had seen a ghost, perhaps not just one.

What she had seen riding her bike around the city wasn't good.

"They are chasing everyone out of Phnom Penh. They are saying that anyone who resists will be shot. The soldiers are

---

[2] He did return eventually, but lived under house arrest for the entire regime. Many of his family, including children and grandchildren, were slaughtered.

only children with guns!"

Mama went over to Grandma Lee's and explained that in the western parts of the city, where the Khmer Rouge had first entered, people were already being ordered to leave. Ever practical, she suggested that Grandma take her stock of Khmer fabrics with her, as they would be valuable in the villages. Grandma didn't want to leave and she and her family spent some time trying to hide things under the staircase. She also wanted my father to stay behind with her, but by midday Mama has us packed and ready to go and she was not in the mood to negotiate.

Uncle Yu, who had by this time graduated from university, now worked for a gold dealer who lived in front of our building. She was a widow and he often stayed at her house. Mama asked him to come with us, but the widow wanted him to stay with her and her daughter and two young sons. The adults had started the day relieved the war was over and curious about what was to come, but already those initial emotions had been replaced with fear and confusion.

Not long after lunch the Khmer Rouge arrived in our neighbourhood and started going from block to block and house to house, telling us loudly that we all had to leave the city immediately because the Americans were about to bomb us. A few young Khmer Rouge *Yothea Padevat* (soldiers of the revolution) with grenade launchers and AK47 rifles casually slung over their shoulders, stood in our alley urging us along, saying, "Hurry up, get out of Phnom Penh. The Americans are going to bomb the city. There is no need to take anything with you. You'll be back in a few days, maybe even tomorrow. Hurry up. Leave now. America is going to bomb the city!"

They told us to leave our belongings because we would be back in a few days - or as soon as they finished checking our houses for hidden enemies. The atmosphere became confused and suspicious. Why would there be an enemy hiding in our house? It did not make sense, but we didn't dare question their authority because they all held guns. People loaded their trolleys, carts, whatever they had with cash and clothes.

Because of Mama's forethought we were already prepared to leave. She did not have to worry about taking money because she had stocked up on goods before the curfews started. Mama was instantly suspicious about them saying they had to search our houses: ours were so small, just four-by-four metre concrete boxes, it would take only moments, not days to go right through them. She believed we would be gone for a few weeks, perhaps even a few months. Mama somehow knew that there was no point trying to reason with these gun-toting kids. The younger ones were too quiet, their faces emotionless, while the older ones were too angry, shouting orders, preparing to herd us along. We were being driven from the city, not knowing our destination. Mama's main concern was whether we would be away so long that I and the other children would get hungry and cold in the impending rainy season. We had a hand trolley loaded with canned food and other merchandise which she'd organised a week before when the market had still been open. She now added rice, cooking utensils and bowls, spoons and knives which hung from the side, as well as our clothes and some spare *Krama* and sarongs. She also planned to take her priceless family photo album.

"What are you doing with that?" Father asked.

"I want to take it. You don't know how long we will be away or when can we come back!"

"Bah, they said we'll only be gone for a few days."

Mama didn't say anything, but she stashed it away in the bottom of the trolley so that Father didn't know.

I didn't realise it at the time, but that day in April was to mark the end of my childhood. I was too young to understand that it was not the beginning of free Cambodia, at last released from the colonial restraint of both the French and the Americans, as well as the triumphant return of the King Father we had been promised[3], but the start of something far more sinister. I did not realise that I would soon see the end of my

---

[3] He was allowed to return to Phnom Penh, but remained under house arrest for the duration of the regime.

freedom for a long time. I could not have imagined what was about to happen.

Until the war, things had been getting better for my family. We had just welcomed my third younger brother, Hun, only a few months earlier. Mama had been able to take some time off work now that Yu and Hiam were old enough to run the stall. Father had taken Mama and my younger brothers on a day trip to Angkor Wat. He had also taken me in his white Mercedes to visit the old French resort on top of Mt Bok Kor in southern Cambodia. Like many children of my age, life had been relatively peaceful and innocent. I should have been running around in the playground playing with toys or having a game of hide-and-seek, attending school and learning.

From that day in April playgrounds and schools became luxurious memories of the past. The family's comfortable lifestyle that Mama had been working so hard to build for more than ten years came to an abrupt stop. Like so many others that day, only bitterness and hardship lay ahead of us.

Mama carried my youngest brother over her shoulder in a *Krama* and while carrying a gallon of drinking water in her right hand. I had a few small belongings hung onto my little bicycle. Father tied a *Krama* to the heavy food trolley and hooked the scarf over his shoulder while Hiam, Huang and Chong pushed from behind. This is how we started heading towards the outskirt of Phnom Penh. One by one, families from our block stepped out into the alley and started walking towards the Wat Ounalom exit. I took one last look at the house. Lily was standing near doorstep, looking like she was holding back tears, swaying her head from side to side in confusion.

"Mama, what about Lily and her puppies?" I asked.

"They have to stay here. We can't take them with us," she replied sadly.

Lily wagged her tail as fast as she could as if she was begging me to come back. She was pacing quickly back and forth, back and forth, torn between whether to stay with her puppies or to follow us. She disappeared back into the house just as we started moving.

I had so many questions, but there were no answers. Why did we have to leave our home? Where were we going? What would happen to Lily and her puppies? Who would look after my Siamese fish that I had hidden in the dark corner under my bed? I couldn't ask Mama or Father as they were too busy dragging the trolley along the crowded street in the heat and humidity. It was hard to push even my bike through the crowd. We could hardly move. Mama was trying to spot Uncle Yu and Grandma Lee in the sea of people emerging under the shadow of the Pepsi Cola factory. We waited as long as we could for Yu, but the soldiers were yelling at us and we were afraid that they might start shooting. We followed the crowd, there was only one direction to move: south and out of the city. Crowds of people from every direction all heading the same way. We finally understood: the entire population of Phnom Penh, which had swelled to over two million since the war had begun, was being evacuated. Then, amazingly, I saw Lily, happily wagging her tail, following in my footsteps. A dog's instinct to find her owner.

"Mama, Lily is here," I told Mama.

"Shoo! Shoo!" Mama stamped her feet and waved her hands up and down trying to chase Lily back home to her puppies, but she refused to obey. She kept following, somehow managing to avoid being crushed by all the tramping feet. She had made her choice and left her three puppies. There was no way of sending her back, we had to keep moving, even if it was only a few centimetres at a time. By sunset we had walked less than two kilometres. Thousands and thousands of us were all heading toward the main highways. Somehow, in the crowd near the Buddhist shrine, we caught up with Grandma's family. Uncle Yu, sadly, was still nowhere to be found. Presumably he had gone in a different direction. Grandma and her family joined us and we settled down near the shrine to rest for the evening. Mother boiled water for our instant noodles in American military canteen cups shaped like big peanuts. All around us people were camping and cooking along the roadside. We spread a mattress on the ground and soon after dinner I fell asleep, tired from the heat and the walk.

The next day and the day after that we woke up early to take advantage of the cooler conditions and continued our journey at the same pace. The air became thick and dusty from so many people dragging their feet along the dirty streets in the April heat. Each day we advanced only a few kilometers at best as the heat became unbearable by midday and we would take shelter under the trees while Mama prepared lunch. We'd start moving again in the late afternoon, walking late into the evening. Some people pushed trolleys and bicycles like us, others had small carts or wore yokes over their shoulders. Some women carried things on their heads. Rich people with cars were forced to abandon them because the roads were too crowded. Every now and then I heard gunshots behind us, a sign that we needed to move faster. It took us nearly a week to walk along the Bassac River.

There was no indication we would be returning home. We were surrounded by people as far as the eye could see. For many of them food and water were already running low, and there were no toilet facilities. We had to do it on street corners or anywhere we could find privacy. There was a foul smell of urine and faeces all along the road, sometimes combined with the smell of decaying animals. People rested right on the footpath exhausted from the heat and lack of food. Others walked all night, hoping that by getting out of the city as quickly as possible they might reach freedom - or even just survive. Eventually we reached the outskirts of Phnom Penh and crossed the Bassac River at the Kbal Thnoul Bridge on the southern side of the city. It had taken us a week to travel six kilometres.

Before we crossed over the bridge, the Khmer Rouge instructed us to spend all our money. We were told that money wasn't used in the provinces anymore, whether riels or dollars, and that if we tried it would put our lives in danger. Mama, who was already worried about mosquitoes, didn't argue and spent 40,000 riels on a net which had been only a few hundred riels a month earlier. She spent another 20,000 on a litre of cooking oil. Six months ago, that amount could have bought two ounces of gold! Because of Mama's quick thinking we had enough food to last us a couple of months. Ever the woman with an eye for a bargain, she would exchange some of our food for other things we needed if necessary. Someone offered her two ounces of gold for fifteen kilos of rice, but she said no. She wasn't going to give up her rice that easily. All the shops and warehouses along the road had been abandoned and were now empty, having been looted by those fleeing the city very early on. Even I had joined the crowd on one occasion, managing to pick up a few boxes of instant noodles. Having money didn't guarantee food anymore. A Mercedes abandoned on the road had a trunk full of five hundred riel notes. No one wanted them. The basic items of life, like salt and rice, became more valuable than diamonds and pearls. A man tried to swap his watch for my looted noodles. I said no.

After crossing the Bassac River, we continued our exodus along Highway 1. We now knew this was a one-way trip as the Khmer Rouge *Yothea* (soldiers) were telling us we needed to go to our family villages. We walked through small towns along the way, all as empty as Phnom Penh. The houses were deserted and everything valuable was gone. Any place considered a centre of capitalism had been evacuated. The schools and temples were quiet. These towns had been controlled by the Khmer Rouge before the war ended, so they had been emptied months previously.

We continued to move slowly inland, resting when we could under trees or beneath the verandas of abandoned houses. We cooked and ate on the side of the road. Our toilet was behind whatever convenient bush or tree we could find. We woke up every morning to the unpleasant smells around us, noisy footsteps and muted conversations and the sounds of pots and pans dangling from the sides of carts. I wished it was a dream. I no longer had a bed. I hadn't slept underneath a roof since that morning when the war ended. The leaves were my roof for now. And there was much worse to come my worst nightmare had just begun.

CHAPTER FIVE

A FORK IN THE ROAD

A couple more weeks passed. We eventually reached another former market town, called Korki, about twenty-five kilometres from the city and the final checkpoint on Highway 1. Sadly, Uncle Yu was still nowhere to be seen among the thousands and thousands of people camped here. Although there were more people arriving from the city every day, there were still some who hoped we would soon be sent back home. I don't know why they thought that. Perhaps they just couldn't take it in. The Khmer Rouge kept telling us we had to return to village of our birth, our hometown. I could understand the confusion: my birthplace was twenty-five kilometres behind us! Mama knew they were up to something. She had seen those young Khmer Rouge *Yothea* rounded up Lon Nol's soldiers and took them away. She realised that once we arrived in our village, the local Khmer Rouge would recognise us, would know our family history and what we had been doing in Phnom Penh. Perhaps there was a chance for old grudges to be settled. Mama could sense danger. She said, "Where I've come from, in a small village, everyone knows everyone else too well. There is no way to hide your family history in your birth village. The villagers know you and what you did in the old days. They know if you're rich or poor, or whether you're educated. They know if your father was a policeman or a high ranking general." Mother warned those families around us who had connections to the government not to return home. Her gut feeling told her that any form of connection to the government would be enough cause for arrest and imprisonment, including those in the Cambodian army who had thrown away their uniforms after the fall of the city. Already there were whispers that the Khmer Rouge had taken some families away because of perceived or actual military connections - and who knew if they would be seen again?

It was time for a decision. We had been travelling east along the highway, but now we had a choice to turn north or south. Taking the wrong turn could mean death. Despite our concerns and worry about the danger, we had limited options. Except for Mama, Yu and Hiam, Phnom Penh was the hometown of the rest of us, including Father. Mama felt we had nothing to conceal, so we decided to head north to her village of Kor near Prey Torteng where we could stay at her parent's house with her brothers and sisters.

Another consideration was that after almost a month of walking and pushing the trolley, Mama just wanted to be at a place where we could settle down as soon as possible. Waiting at Korki trying to work out what the Lee families wanted to do would put more strain on our rapidly dwindling food supply. They couldn't make up their minds, and still held out hope that we would be allowed to return to Phnom Penh. We had to decide before the food was gone. No one was bartering anymore, we were all holding onto what we had brought with us. Bags of gold were worth as much as birds in the bush, cash was only good for toilet paper. Banknotes whirled with in dust on the side of the highway in the last heat of the dry season.

While we were camping at Korki, Mama would sometimes run into our neighbours from Kandal Market. She would ask if they had seen Uncle Yu, and tell them to pass on a message to him if they did. "Tell him we're staying underneath that mango tree over there," she'd say, pointing to where our trolley was. "If we're not there, we're going home to Kor."

Then, good luck! Right in the middle of the crowd of people at Korki we spotted Yu on his bike, just as if he'd arrived from out of thin air. He was still with the widow, but Mama persuaded him to come with us. Mama was thrilled to see him again, doubly so knowing we were planning to move on the next day. If we hadn't have come across him that day perhaps we never would have. Having Yu with us meant we had another adult who could help haul the heavy trolley with Father - although it also meant we had another mouth to feed.

Grandma Lee and her family were all ethnic Chinese who

had been born in Phnom Penh, except for Grandfather who was from China. They had only ever lived in Phnom Penh. They had no village to go to, so they wanted to head south hoping to find shelter in Vietnam as Grandma had some relatives in Saigon. Grandma wanted us to come with them, but Mama refused. Once again Grandma was not going to let go so easily. She insisted that my father went with her. Mama told her that he was welcome to - but only if he left his wife and children behind. Father was a sensible man and he decided to stay with Mama. If he had wanted to leave us, he could have hopped onto the helicopter and been in America by now. In the end, Grandma Lee, Grandpa and their two single daughters, Aunt Hun and Heng, Muy and her family and Small Uncle and his family all headed south for the border. There were stories that people who had left earlier had entered Vietnam already.

Father also had another younger brother, Uncle Yuen (who had a family of six children) who had been living at Pochentong. They had come to stay at Kandal Market with Grandma after the airport was bombed and had been stuck there ever since. Because of this they didn't have many belongings with them. During the evacuation, Yuen's wife had often argued with Muy at meal times because they had so little to contribute. They now decided to head west, wanting to get back to Pochentong, although Mama knew this would be impossible. She tried to stop them and asked them to come with us, but they refused and there were more arguments.

In the middle of all the confusion, chaos and exhaustion, Father had become very quiet. He seemed to have lost all sense of feeling. He didn't talk about what this separation would mean to him - he didn't know whether we were ever going to see each other again. At meal times, he would sit by himself and silently eat his bowl of rice and dry fish. It was heart breaking for him to see his family on each other - the circumstances were difficult enough as it was. Although he showed no emotion, a few more wrinkles had appeared and somehow his eyes were deeper set than they had been. Grandma implored him one last time to join her, but he shook his head, no. Since he and Mama had moved out of Grandma's house they were considered inferior, and the distance between my family and Grandma's had grown wider. It was always Mama, the country Khmer girl and them, the city Chinese. So, it was that we split up and went our separate ways.

The clouds were dark and laden, monsoon season was near. We were back on the road. Once again, we had to make do with what we had and deal with being without basic services, like sanitation. If I wanted to go to the toilet I would walk a couple metres away from the road, take down my pants and squat. Before I had finished, the flies would flock in, tickling me on my bare skin and annoying me. I would try and wiggle my bottom to get them away. After I finished, I would pick a few leaves to wipe myself with and to cover what I had left behind.

The monsoon finally arrived just as we turned off the highway onto an unpaved, muddy road. We were looking for a ferry to take us across the Mekong River. We were now surrounded by rice paddies. The fields were empty and the farmers' houses were deserted. It was the season when the fields should have been full of people planting the new rice crop, but there was no one there.

The rain made it more humid, but it also washed away the smells we had known for so long. It washed the accumulated human waste from the sides of the highway into the paddy fields. The conditions would make the ground rich, but for now only for grass.

One day I went into a field looking for somewhere to go to the toilet when I stumbled on a corpse. It was swollen, dark green and purple, lying alone on the bank of a paddy. I guessed it must have been there for many days. Judging from the sarong I guessed she was Khmer. Perhaps the poor soul had died of illness or starvation. Presumably there had been no time for anyone to bury her. Her face was rotten beyond recognition and her eyes were gone. I wondered how I could have seen it before smelling it because now the smell was so thick it was choking me. I felt it would linger on my clothes for days if I stayed any longer. Then I realised there was a sound as well, the buzzing of thousands of green-headed flies all feasting on her. I realised she was full of maggots. I felt like vomiting, my mouth was sour with the taste of the green mango I had had for lunch. This was the first dead body I had ever seen. I shivered as I realised what the smell that had been lingering in the air around us was. I had seen sick and exhausted people as we walked, now I realised that some of them had stayed where they had fallen. The smell was not normal, but these were not normal times, no one had the time to care, to show the proper respect, we were just travelling along, trying to reach our unwanted destinations.

By this time, we had been walking for more than a month. If we'd been able to leave the city from the north, we would already have arrived in my mother's village. If we'd travelled on Highway 6 and 7, instead of Highway 1, we could have walked there within a week. It only took my mother's father half a day on his bike to visit us in Phnom Penh but we'd been forced to take a complete detour around the city. We were exhausted and aware we needed to get to the village before our supplies ran out. A new threat emerged: people were starting to steal from each other.

This meant that the adults, including Yu and Hiam, had to take turns to stay awake and guard the trolley. We were lucky because we had Lily with us, and she would bark at anyone who came near. Not that we were sleeping that well, and we only had the one mosquito net to share, the one Mama had bought with the last of our paper money. Each evening we would set it up under a handy tree: mango or tamarind were the best. We only took shelter underneath the eaves of an abandoned house if it was raining. With the arrival of the monsoon our progress slowed even more as it was hard to travel when it was wet.

The food was the same every day. I was getting bored with boiled rice, canned sardines and green mango salad, sometimes with the addition of dry smoked river fish that Mama had bought just before the markets closed. There was no fresh meat or vegetables apart from the mangoes we found on the trees or young tamarind leaves. The trees should have been full of mangoes ripening on the branches, not surprisingly there were hardly any left, just those right up high that were hard to reach. The tamarind trees had started sprouting their young light green leaves which we used to make Khmer sour soup. Back in Phnom Penh Mama would have added lemon grass and lime leaves, sugar and fish sauce along with a handful of Morning Glory, some chopped green tomato and pineapple, but now all she could do was boil the leaves and add salt. There was no fresh mint, chilli or salted crab. There was nothing!

Every day our bag of rice was growing lighter and lighter. We were too exhausted to move any faster, the best we could do was manage a couple of kilometres a day - and every day on the road meant we had one day less of food.

The rain and the mud meant the end for my little bike. Its tyres had gone flat and it was too hard and slippery to push it along. I was lagging behind and complaining, jealous of my younger brothers riding on the trolley and my father eventually made the decision to leave it behind.

Hearing that the Khmer Rouge had evacuated the city, my grandfather on my mother's side, Kong Huot (Grandfather Huot), and my mother's brothers had earlier started searching for us along Highways 6 and 7. They spent weeks on their bikes going as far as Prek Kdam on the Tonle Sap River. Sadly, we were still on the other side of the city so they didn't find us. They finally gave up and went back home, hoping we would one day turn up.

Gradually the crowds started to thin as people diverged into different parts of the country. There were no cars anymore, the last of these had been abandoned at Korki. Although it was easier to walk along the less crowded roads, our footsteps were heavier and our trolley wheels were squeakier and full of clay mud. By late May, however, when we finally arrived at a ferry which could take us across the Mekong River, we found yet more chaos. Everyone had converged here desperate to get across before the peak of the monsoon hit or perhaps before they ran out of food. The waters of the

FATHER MISSED HIS PLANE

Mekong River were rising, and so was the death toll. Many had starved, and some now chose to end their lives in the river than live another day without food. There were thousands of people but only a few small boats to take us across the muddy water. We waited days, eating into our dwindling food supply, but eventually Mama found us a boat. There were so few each day, and they didn't all stop at every destination. Mother heard that a boat was going to a place called Prey Torteng, and she wasted no time rounding us up.

"Go, go! This is the boat we want. We need to get on it now!" she shouted. Prey Torteng wasn't far from Mama's village. We rushed for the boat. In a matter of minutes, it was fully packed. It didn't take us long to realise that it was over capacity. The Khmer Rouge who were watching us didn't care that it was overloaded. While we were all concerned, it could sink, none of us were prepared to disembark either - it might be the only boat across the river for a long time.

Father and I stood on the edge of the deck, Mama and the rest of the family were somewhere in the middle, as the little diesel engine started and we pulled away from the riverbank. Tok-Tok, Tok-Tok. We held on tight to an iron pole holding up a small canopy. Father gave me instructions, worried that the boat would capsize. He was scared because he had four young children to take care of and none of us could swim. He emptied our drinking water from a plastic container and handed it to me. He told me to hold on tight to it if the boat sank and he would rescue me as soon as he could. I believed him. He was a good swimmer as his grandfather had owned a fishing farm and he had spent his childhood playing in the river. He could swim across the 300 metres plus width of the Tonle Sap River without difficulty.

I was prepared for the worst. The small boat had more than a hundred people on it, and many would die if it capsized. Slowly and steadily it made its way upstream and toward the far bank. It zigged and it zagged and struggled against the current for more than two hours. It was so low in the water that large waves sometimes splashed onto the deck. Finally, we saw the distant shore approaching, but it took almost another hour before we finally docked.

We got off the boat as quickly as we could and resumed our trek to the village. The roads here were even more rough, muddy and slippery, and there was still another twenty-five kilometres to go. It was hard going to push the trolley along. The good thing about having nearly run out of food was that it made the trolley much lighter. That first evening after we crossed the river Mama decided we should rest in an abandoned house for a few nights to regain our strength before setting off again. None of us disagreed with her.

Meanwhile Grandfather Huot had run into one of his relatives who had seen us on the road. "We met Lay-Ourn and her family on the other side. Yu and Hiam are with them," she told my grandfather.

They discussed where the most likely place for us to cross the river was, and my grandfather packed some food and set out to search for us once again. It must have been a miracle, because although it had been raining solidly for days, Mama heard it stop and went outside to look around. And what was the first thing she saw?!

"Pa, Pa!" she shouted, seeing her father on his bike. They found each other in the middle of nowhere! Grandfather Huot was so happy - he had been looking for us for a long time. He was very anxious and worry that he would never see us at all. When Mama called out for us to come out to meet him, I could hear the relief in his voice as he greeted us. "I had been looking for all of you everywhere on the other side for days", he exclaimed with excitement and waved his hands up and down and from side to side to reinforce that he had been everywhere to look for us.

As if this miracle wasn't enough, along came one of his neighbours with an ox cart from nowhere asking if we needed help to get back home. In those early days of the regime villagers were still able to travel, and some had taken to helping the refugees, albeit in exchange for food or clothing. Mama recognized the driver, he was an old friend from the village and we gladly accepted his offer. We loaded what few belongings we still had left, threw away the hand trolley and off we went, led by Grandfather Huot on his bike.

It was the first time I had ridden on an ox wagon and it was quite an experience. The pair of light brown oxen had yokes over their shoulders, and the bells hanging from their necks rang to the motion of their heads moving up and down as they pulled the wagon forward. We rocked and swayed along the muddy clay paths through the rice fields, hitting small bumps every now and then. It made my tired body feel even more lethargic. I fell asleep and when I woke up it was evening and we had arrived at Kor Village. Mama offered the driver some of our old clothes and a can of sardines in tomato sauce, because that was all we had to offer. He was very happy with the exchange, and we were more than grateful for the ride because without those sturdy oxen, it would have taken us a long time to get there.

Our time away from the city was never meant to be just for a few days. The intention of the Khmer Rouge had always been to evacuate us permanently from the city to start their agrarian ideal, one where fruits and crops were grown on the farms, and stayed on the farms. There were no more cities or marketplaces because they were symbols of the capitalist: places where people were corrupt and exploitative. The Khmer Rouge had lied to us from the moment they entered the city. They had forced us from our homes, confiscating watches when they saw them so no one could tell the time, and radios so we had no communication with the outside world. We were cut off and no one had any idea what we were going through. There were no enemies hiding in our houses. There were no imperialist planes dropping bombs. There were no Americans waiting to invade. The Americans and their helicopters were long gone. It had taken us more than a month to reach Mama's village. At long last Father could sit down and rest, leaning back against the trunk of the coconut tree in front of Grandfather Huot's house. He reached into his front pocket and pulled out his packet of 555-brand cigarettes. He had not smoked for days.

He had been saving the last for this moment. He pulled one out and tapped the butt of the cigarette against the box, his usual habit, before raising it to his dry brown lips and lighting up. He took a long puff, the fire at the tip of the cigarette illuminated the space surrounding his face like a red lantern in the dark. He drew his breathe deep into the lungs; he knew it too well that soon he would not remember the smell and the taste of this 555-brand cigarette. He let the smoke linger in his lungs, enjoying the first breath, before slowly blowing it out through his nose and letting the smoke gently drift away.

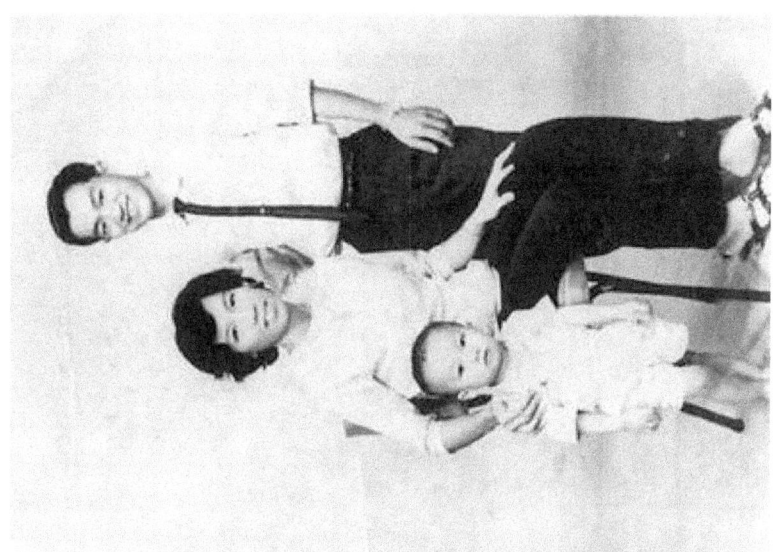

Three Years Old: Me, my mother and father.

Kandal Market, Before 1975
In the Park behind Mama's Market Stall, Huang, Chong and Me.

Father, Huang, Chong and me.

Left to right, Me in my school uniform, Huang and Chong, in front of the white Mercedes my father was hired to drive.

Mama's market stall showing the canned goods she was selling. My brothers Huang and Chong (I'm in the bottom right corner).

Phnom Penh, before 1975: Mama and Hun outside the Kandal Market apartment.

Chapter Six

Angkar Padevat

Many of the residents of Phnom Penh were forced to settle in random villages when they ran out of food or became too exhausted to travel any further. A few more families had also arrived at Kor Village and there were reports that those of the people who had stranded at ferry ports in Korki had been trucked away to remote Northern provinces and continue their long march, so I was very glad we had reached Grandfather Huot's village. Despite the long detour and lack of food we had all survived. As Mama's younger brothers and sisters came to help unload our belongings from the ox cart, we settled into Grandfather Huot's house for the evening.

The next morning Mama's relatives gathered to welcome us. I was happy to meet aunts, uncles and cousins I had never seen before. They were glad that we had arrived safely but also hoped that we had brought some presents from Phnom Penh for them! Mama had always brought gifts whenever she and my father visited the village previously. This time she only had few old clothes and sarongs to offer. They were happy with them, especially the sarongs, which were in much better condition than the ones they were wearing. Their clothes were the same as those worn by the Khmer Rouge, although darker, but they were old and very patched, so new sarongs were in great demand. My parents and relatives talked about what had happened in Phnom Penh and on the road, and also about what had happened once the Khmer Rouge arrived in the village.

The arrival of the Khmer Rouge was the beginning of a new authoritarian regime, the start of a new future. The new leadership referred to themselves as *Angkar Padevat* (the revolutionary organisation). The Khmer Rouge started a new calendar the day they took control, and the starting point - where we were now - was called Year Zero, the beginning of the beginning. Cambodia was going to abolish all wealth, markets, religions, landlords and possessions, and even personal relationships. In the new regime, there was no longer bad and good or negative versus positive or rich against poor, now everything was equal. All debts were cleared and wealth was destroyed to make way for a fresh new society where everyone had to start from zero. People in Kor Village had been told to *Lott Dam* (forge a new revolution) with Angkar. Religion had been outlawed and monks in the village were ordered from the temples to work in the rice fields. In Kor Village and in all the villages, schools, hospitals and markets were shut down. Money was banned and people were expected to exchange what they made or grew for what they wanted. There was no economy other than the barter system. They had turned Cambodia into a classless society, a place where everyone was supposed to be equal. As the province had fallen to the Khmer Rouge long before the war had ended elsewhere, it had been like this for a couple of years already. All land had been confiscated to become part of the Khmer Rouge cooperative farming system. The Khmer Rouge had appointed the local village chief to oversee and implement Angkar's agricultural policy while my grandfather was the representative for the local Chinese committee. The local ethnic Chinese were forced to close their shops and restaurants and work alongside their Khmer neighbours in the paddy fields. The villagers had to collectively farm rice together. The crop was stored in a central warehouse to be distributed after the harvest season based on each household's contribution. A share could come from using your oxen in the field, or the work of your entire family. For us, Grandfather Huot had a pair of oxen, my uncle was a driver and two of my aunts worked in the field.

 Not long after our joyful family reunion, the village chief, the local Khmer Rouge representative and a couple of Khmer Rouge *Yothea* (with their trademark communist caps, *Krama* and AK47s) came over to register us. Even though Mama had been born and raised in the village (as had her parents, and her brothers and sisters who still lived there) we still needed to have our family history recorded and describe what we had been doing in Phnom Penh.

This was our first face to face experience of Angkar. During our journey to the village, Mama had already recognized that whatever Angkar was, it was not kind. She suspected the Khmer Rouge couldn't be trusted. There were many rumours surrounding the fate of all the Cambodian soldiers who had been rounded up after the fall of Phnom Penh. She believed that the Khmer Rouge was killing anyone who had connections with the former government or with America. She had also heard stories of people who had been taken away at checkpoints after giving details of official connections. In addition, Mama heard from Grandfather Huot and her other relatives about the families who had arrived in the village earlier, to then be trucked away somewhere else, far away, on the orders of Angkar. There were questions as to their actual fate. By now we all doubted the official story: that they had been sent for *Korsang* (re-education.)

Mama had told Father to tell our interrogators as little as possible, worried that one wrong revelation could get us in trouble.

"*Mett* (Comrade) must tell Angkar the truth about your history and what *Mett* did in the old regime," the village chief said.

"*Mett*, where did *Mett* come from?"

"How old are *Mett's* sons?"

"Did *Mett* do any work for the government in Lon Nol's regime?"

"What type of business did *Mett* have?"

The chief had known Mama since she was a baby, yet he was asking about her background as if he'd never met her, but that was part of the Khmer Rouge procedures. Mama kept a straight face and explained that she was a stallholder and that my father was a taxi driver. She kept our story simple. We had just been ordinary people struggling to make a living in the big city - which in many ways wasn't far from the truth. She talked about how we'd shared accommodation with Father's relatives, and how the rest of her family, aside from Yu and Hiam, had stayed behind in the village. She still had her village identification card. She also knew how to wear her sarong the village way (Cambodian Chinese in the city usually wore trousers) and could walk with a basket of rice or fruit on her head. She knew so many of the villagers, and they knew her. The Khmer Rouge had no choice but to accept that we were "bona fide" Khmers. It was obvious we had no connections to anyone who used to be in a position of power: no generals or rich merchants. My father was a simple driver who delivered goods or people as required.

What Mama didn't say was that in addition to his taxi, Father had also been a regular chauffeur for one of the Lon Nol's generals. She also didn't tell Angkar that until 1963 Father's identification card had recorded him as Chinese.

It wasn't just Father who had something to hide from Angkar, though. There were two other members of my family who needed to keep their pasts concealed. Uncle Yu had graduated from university, been a hippie and had supported the government backed protests against Vietnam. He would have been seen as an enemy. And there was one other person they would liked to have known about - and that was me, because I had attended the American school. Even speaking a foreign language was enough to have me deemed as an enemy. Khmer was now the only language allowed, to the point that ethnic Chinese people were prohibited from speaking Chinese even at home. If Angkar had found out about any of us we might have been sent for "*Korsang.*"

The Khmer Rouge had a name for those of us who hadn't embraced the regime but who had had it forced upon us: we were *Nyak Tmay* (New People.) We had to discard our old habits, forget the past, embrace the new regime and start a completely new way of life. It was a totally different world. The farmers, peasants and the uneducated were now our superiors while merchants, businessmen and doctors - anyone with an education - were about to be either killed or terrified into complete intellectual surrender. All the people from the cities, even the monks who previously had always been among those granted the highest respect, were now inferior. Grandfather Huot had a Cambodian metaphor for our situation: "Now dry gourds sink and broken pots float!" The world was upside down. The peasants were the rulers and everyone else was in the mud. The village idiot had a better chance of surviving this regime than we did.

After the Khmer Rouge had accepted that we were just another family of common, uneducated street hawkers, Angkar had one other stroke to play: some of our meagre possessions would be confiscated. "*Mett* are now part of Angkar's *Sahakor* (Commune) and everything *Mett* have is part of the cooperative."

Their first target was Uncle Yu's bicycle, but then they also demanded my grandfather's bicycle and his old motorbike. The Khmer Rouge *Yothea* were extremely polite.

"*Mett*, Angkar requests your bikes." It was almost as if they regretted asking us, and were only following Angkar's order - but they were Angkar. Whenever they spoke it was always with reference to Angkar as a disembodied third person. They were giving the orders but it was in the words of Angkar, as Angkar's instruction, or at Angkar's request. They asked if we had any other valuable items such as watches or radios, but Mama had been quick to hide anything that would give away evidence of our status in Phnom Penh, including her precious photo album.

Grandfather Huot was very unhappy about the bikes and turned to the Khmer Rouge *Yothea* with another one of his local metaphors.

"You guys are faster than flies to fresh shit! My daughter's just arrived, her seat isn't even warm yet and you've got your hands out to take everything she has!"

The Khmer Rouge *Yothea* replied politely, "But this is Angkar's request, *Mett*." My grandfather was used to being addressed as *Kong Huot* or *Ta Huot* (Grandfather Huot), now he was simply *Mett*. Grandfather Huot and Grandmother Huot had been born in the village, he was a pig farmer who often represented the local ethnic Chinese community because he spoke Khmer so well. The chief was one of his neighbours and knew Grandfather Huot could be outspoken. If Grandfather Huot had been one of the New People, like we were, he would have been in deep trouble for talking like this against Angkar, and might have been immediately removed for *Korsang*.

It was all very strange for me. I was trying to understand these new terms: *Mett*, Angkar, *Sahakor*, old regime, new regime, Year Zero, New People and so on. One thing I did understand was my grandfather's reference to how quickly flies came to shit. I had never heard this expression before but after two months on the road I had had first-hand experience of its accuracy!

Mama told my grandfather not to argue with Angkar, "Pa, let Angkar take the bicycles." Angkar gratefully accepted our bikes, along with my grandfather's old motorbike, although this wasn't a great concern for us because there was no longer any petrol. Mama had a plan, however, and while my grandfather was arguing she had her brothers remove the motorbike's tyres and hide them. Then she handed over the tyreless motorbike along with our bicycles.

"*Mett*, please take them."

Having grown up in the village Mama knew those old tyres could be cut up to make sandals. I had seen the Khmer Rouge wearing them when they entered Phnom Penh and they were wearing them here, too. They were simple and reliable footwear whether you were walking around the village or in the jungle. The outer tyre was cut to the required size and fit, and then the inner tube was used to make soft straps: two at the front and two at the back. It wasn't long before Mama turned those tyres into new sandals for us.

Angkar ordered all the New People onto small blocks of land on the edge of the village, away from the main road and the locals. They had to build huts with whatever wood, bamboo and palm leaves they could find. Huts were soon scattered everywhere, but fortunately we didn't have to be among them as Grandfather Huot insisted we stayed with him.

His house was large enough to accommodate all of us and fortunately the chief agreed to his request. After the Khmer Rouge and the chief had left, my grandfather wasted no time in cursing them.

"These idiots are taking us back to the stone age. They were born deaf, dumb and blind, and now they are running the country!"

Mama took stock of the goods she had hidden. There were some watches her quick thinking had stashed away back at the first checkpoint when so many other people had had theirs confiscated, there were some ear rings, her treasured photo album, and a watch of Uncle Yu's. She was worried that the Khmer Rouge *Yothea* had already seen it, so she made up a story for him swapping it for ricer if anyone asked.

"Tell them that I swapped it for some rice because we did not have anything to eat," she instructed Uncle Yu.

Since the market was closed we had to rely on Grandfather Huot's rice and the sweet potatoes and other vegetables he grew in his small back garden. We didn't know whether we would be here for next year's harvest or if we would be able to return to Phnom Penh once the Khmer Rouge had completed their "inspection." We were concerned because Grandfather Huot was running very low on food - there had been five in the house before we arrived, now there were thirteen, which meant there wasn't going to be enough to last. We started to ration it, but this meant our daily meals always left us hungry. Grandmother had always dried out and stored leftover rice to give to the pigs, now she fed it to us. Sometimes she used the soft young centres of banana trees to supplement our already thin porridge. She minced the young banana trees and cooked them with the rice to make the porridge thicker. This was an ingredient that Kong Huot used to mix up for the pigs. It was all there was. We were eating pig food!

Mama had no choice but to trade what was left of our clothes and Papa's Rolex watch for a few kilos of unhusked rice from the neighbours. To keep us going until the next harvest, which was still six months away, we cooked it as porridge rather than as boiled rice - it went further. The only thing we could add to the rice was what we could find in the paddies like crabs, frogs, snails and catfish. I spent all my days looking for crab holes, all too often it was only the holes I found, and no crabs. Any easily available food had been taken long ago.

When we finally ran out, Grandfather Huot realised he now had a great excuse to slaughter one of his pigs. But he needed permission from Angkar. The situation in the village had changed very rapidly. In a matter of weeks, all bartering was forbidden and even if it was permissible anyone with food was now holding tightly to it. The only place that still had plenty of rice was the Angkar's warehouses.

"I'll go and ask the chief, and if he says yes we'll have some pork but we'll also have enough left over to trade for rice."

The pigs were now the only item of value left in the family. There were two of them and he'd had them for more than two years and they weighed about 200 kilos each. The chief had stopped Grandfather Huot killing them previously, wanting him to trade the pigs to Angkar in exchange for calico, the plain white cotton fabric which they dyed black to make their uniforms.

"I don't have any food and there's two pigs in the barn! I have to ask those idiots for permission to slaughter my own pigs in my own backyard. I've asked them many times already, but the idiots won't let me!" he said.

He'd kept them at home and fed them for two years and I could feel his frustration as he went to ask for permission to slaughter them because his family was starving.

The chief relented and said yes - but only if Grandfather Huot gave Angkar the other pig in exchange for the cloth. Grandfather Huot was very clever, he managed to get them to agree to throw in a few kilograms of salt and some dried fish as well. As it turned out, the fish were mouldy and full of maggots, and Grandmother had to soak them for half a day to get rid of the smell and a rather oily flavour before she could cook them, but the salt was very useful and Grandmother used it to preserve the pork. My grandfather and his neighbour chopped up the pig. Mama's family were given pieces, as were other members of the neighbourhood cooperative, who gave us two kilograms of unhusked rice in exchange for a kilo of pork - and of course the chief had to be given his share as well.

Then the cooking started. After so long being hungry, the smell of pork belly being seasoned by Grandmother with tamarind and lemon grass made our tummies rumble continuously, loud and clear as if there was thunder. It was like a festival. Because it was special we were going to have boiled rice as well. I circled around that cooking pot like a starving calf at feeding time. My mouth was watering and I could hardly wait. None of us wanted to wait. When it was finally ready, Huang, Chong and our aunts and uncles, we lined up one after another with our plates of rice to receive the hot curry. It was heaven! However, for the New People, this was the beginning of hell.

By this time the village population had grown by more than 200 new families, each with an average of seven people, and hunger soon became a serious issue - especially because so many of the New People had no farming experience. Many had arrived with little food and few possessions or skills to trade with. Starvation and death soon became a real possibility for them. Our family was in a slightly better position because of what Mama had brought with us and because of my grandfather's existing food supplies. With the pigs now gone, though, we knew we would only good for a little while - and what would happen after it finally ran out was impossible to say.

Chapter Seven

From Zero to Nothing

1975, in the middle of the first monsoon season of the regime, Angkar started to implement its vision of a strict "utopian" society. We were all summoned to attend an Angkar *Anprachum Chivapheap* (Livelihood Meeting). These meetings had become part of the routine by now, brainwashing New People with continual propaganda. They were *Anprachum* or meetings where any criticism was met with punishment - some families were taken away after speaking out about their living conditions and never seen again. Those of us with Chinese heritage, especially Father who had first-hand experience, knew about the meetings already, because China Communist had also used them to great effect to brainwash people facing harsh communal labour conditions with very limited rations. The Chinese Communist called it "LaoDong" meaning labour work.

This meeting was different because we were told that Angkar was about to take full control of our lives. The organisation was to assume ultimate power over us and our destinies, including what clothes we'd wear, what food we'd eat and where we'd live. Travel, relationships and even the language we spoke was now all under Angkar's control.

Despite their youth and lack of education, the Khmer Rouge *Yothea* lectured us on how to speak Khmer as if they were using phrases that only scholars could comprehend. They altered the language so we had to learn a whole new vocabulary. It was far more basic than the old one. They abolished traditional forms of expression and replaced them with colloquial peasant terms. Ancient Khmer greetings and terms of respect were banned. Like the way Angkar eliminated the rich and the poor, we no longer needed to address each other as Mr, Mrs, Sir or Madam. Even the word "You" was frowned upon. All of them were replaced with the generic *Mett*.

Ironically *Mett* was one half of the word *Mettphak*, meaning friendship, but Angkar didn't have any friends, only *Mett*.

Angkar even renamed the chief; he was now Chief of the S*ahakor* (commune) instead of village. This pretension towards linguistic control was unfortunately based on nothing. Except for common phrases their language was rough and ignorant, that of the uneducated. They were just children from poor families who had never been to school - and now they were telling us what to do.

The Khmer language is one of the oldest in the world. It is nuanced and structured. Its vocabulary and tone define a speaker's and listener's social status. If you address someone of a certain age, of a certain level of seniority, wealth, rank, religion or gender, very specific words must be used. Despite their Khmer roots, the Khmer Rouge *Yothea* were forgoing the traditional language of centuries. It was worse than that - they were replacing evolved words with rustic plainspeak. They were using expressions I had never heard used in Phnom Penh. There was no more rank, seniority, religion or respect. Every term of address now implied equal status. You could be as old as my grandfather and command the same respect as a two-year-old. Instead of the polite, senior manner I had known, we all had to use the one simple word, *Mett*.

During our registration, my father unintentionally addressed the village chief as *Lok*, meaning Sir, which was the proper way to address someone in a position of authority. The Khmer Rouge told Father not to use this kind of language anymore.

"In this new regime, we don't have any more Sir or Madam."

As a child, I was no longer allowed to use the word *Mae* or Mama, instead I was supposed to call my mother *Mak*, the Khmer Rouge term.

The same rule now also applied to the verb "to eat." There are many ways to express this phrase depending on who you are addressing and their relative age: we had *Nyam* for children, *Pipsah* for elders, *Chun* for monks and commonly *Shi* for anyone within the same age or social status. The Khmer Rouge wanted us to use just one word: *Hoap* (consume) which I had also never heard of before. The Khmer Rouge had put these rules in place in the village when they took over, but most of the older people, like my grandfather, had ignored them. Now no one dared to use the old ways in front of the Khmer Rouge.

One place where equality wasn't demonstrated, however, was in the village. Here there were undeniably two classes: New People and Old People. Anyone who had come from Phnom Penh was "new", while the established villagers, peasants and farmers were "old." Some of them had never been out of the village. Despite Mama's connection to the village, we were "new", while Grandfather Huot and his family were "old". Angkar imposed stricter conditions onto the New People than the locals who were *Nyak Jah* (Old People.)

A travel ban was now also put in place. Until this time people had been able to visit neighbouring villages to trade goods, but this was now forbidden. Barter in this form was too much like the old way. Travelling without permission would cost you your food rights. We realised this was why they had been so eager to confiscate our bikes when we first arrived. Bikes meant we could move faster.

Besides changing our language and who we could see, the Khmer Rouge also instructed us to dress differently. Trousers and shirts had to be black, with no flares, lace or colour. The only exception was the red checkered scarf we had to wear around our head, neck or waist. All my nice clothes from Phnom Penh had to be dyed black - Mama used a mixture of mud and the juice of some dark berries. Of course, it kept washing out, so she had to keep re-dyeing them. Black clothes and used tyre-sandals were the latest (compulsory) fashion in the village. Shirts had to be loose and not tucked in. One afternoon I was with some friends, *Mett*, who were cooking up a stew from a cat they had caught the night before when a New Person walked passed. Perhaps he was insane or had a death wish, because he was wearing a brightly coloured shirt tucked into his burgundy bell bottomed trousers, his belt buckled tightly. We laughed as he walked past us. I never saw him again.

At the *Anprachum* (meeting) the Khmer Rouge told the village that it was nearly time to start planting rice, and that we must all participate if we wished to get food rations from the commune. No *Mett* was allowed to abstain while other *Mett* were working, from the elderly to five-year-old children. Grandmothers were ordered to attend the vegetable gardens and take care of toddlers while their parents were sent to the rice fields. Old men, like my grandfather, looked after the pigs. Angkar set up a roster which told us when to work, eat and sleep. Our communal duty was to rebuild our nation. Angkar would take care of us. Hooray! Hooray! Hooray! But we had no choice other than to participate - because if we didn't we would starve to death.

The village workforce was segregated into different groups. Single men and women were divided and sent to work in fields further away from the village, men in one group and women in another. They were known as *Krom Chalat* (mobile brigades.) People - Yu and Hiam included - were separated from their families and had to stay in remote camps. Young boys and girls were also divided, only kids under five, couples and the elderly worked in the fields near the village.

Then without warning we were prohibited from cooking at home. A lot of people, particularly the elderly, were naturally unhappy about this, but we knew better than to challenge the order. To do so would be to become an enemy of Angkar and that would mean being sent away. This was a terrifying prospect, because anyone who was sent away never returned. There were rumours, of course, that they were being killed, executed in remote forests, but although we suspected this was happening we had not yet witnessed any actual atrocities near the village.

Yet another freedom - a family having a meal at home - was taken away, and was replaced with a communal village kitchen where everyone ate. We were all shocked.

Soon after the meeting the following day, the Khmer Rouge visited my grandfather and told him he didn't need such a large house anymore, since so many of his children would be living in camps. He was to be given the honour of demolishing it so that the timber could be used to build the new kitchen. Most of the other houses in the village were made of bamboo, palm and straw, but ours was solid wood with a proper tin roof that didn't need replacing every year or two like the thatched roofs nearly everyone else had. It wasn't just my grandfather's house - other large homes also owned by ethnic Chinese in the village were also to be knocked down.

This was not the first time the Khmer Rouge had required a house from my grandfather. His sister's house had been empty since she had moved away some time previously, and the Khmer Rouge had persuaded him to "donate" it to become an Angkar palm sugar warehouse.

Now they wanted his own place as well. He was furious.

"This is my *house*! You can't just come and knock it down! Where are we going to live? I already gave you my sister's house. Angkar is taking everything!"

Some people would have been sent away immediately for challenging Angkar, but because he was Old People, and known to the chief, Grandfather Huot was able to get away with it - although this didn't mean he was going to win the argument.

"*Mett*, this house belongs to Angkar now," he was told. "It's Angkar's property and Angkar wants us to demolish it so we can use the wood."

They spoke calmly and reasonably. Again, *they* were Angkar but they spoke like Angkar was someone else and they were just acting on Angkar's behalf.

Mama stepped in.

"It's OK, Pa, Angkar can have the house. We'll find another place."

She turned to one of the Khmer Rouge *Yothea*.

"*Mett*, please come and knock down our house whenever it is suitable for *Mett*."

Just like the time they had come for our bikes, Mama knew we had no hope of keeping the house - her only concern was that we should keep our lives. She quietly explained to my grandfather that if he refused Angkar's request they would probably execute all of us - and Angkar would take the house anyway. We were moved to a palm leaf sided hut down the road, the same as so many others. Angkar said no one should live better than anyone else, and that all *Mett* must be equal. My grandfather stood there silently as he watched a group of local carpenters take down his house, timber by timber, the house that he had lived in all his life.

Grandfather Huot loathed them, and I believe he would have fought back if it wasn't for fear of what would happen to the rest of us. This fear was how they controlled us, how they controlled every soul in the village. We knew by now that their promises of food and that Angkar would take care of us meant nothing. They were not to be trusted. They were sinister and evil, but they had control over us.

The communal kitchen was thought of favourably by those without food of their own, however the reality was that they were now starving, some too weak to even lift a spoon to feed themselves. The field labour combined with malnutrition was causing many deaths. Disease was rife, and many New People succumbed during that first monsoon season. Naturally, Angkar did not believe in doctors or modern medicine. They had destroyed all the hospitals. Instead they offered us herbal medicines of their own, brown balls which looked like rabbit droppings - which is what we called them amongst ourselves. If someone was ill, we'd tell them to go and ask for some rabbit poo. It didn't seem to matter what you were sick with. Headache? Have some rabbit poo. Diarrhoea? Poo. Malaria? Well, more poo, of course. Sadly, without proper care, many died from diarrhoea and malaria, particularly children. We had some traditional remedies of our own, however, such as the one we used for Aunt Hiam's migraines - morning dew collected from the roof of a hut and drunk first thing in the morning. My younger brother, Huang, suffered from night blindness. As soon as it grew dark he couldn't see a thing and I had to lead him to the toilet. This was a symptom of Vitamin A deficiency, although the villagers called the condition "Blind

Chicken" because chickens also can't see after dark. (It's true, I have walked into a chicken coop at night and stood inches away from them with them ignoring me.) The cure for night blindness was to eat a chicken liver, so Grandfather Huot wandered the village hoping to see someone killing a chicken. He then had to quietly ask for the liver, which he would grill on charcoal for Huang.

"Eat this liver, it will cure your Blind Chicken problem," said Grandfather Huot.

Sure enough, after eating chicken livers for a while, Huang's eyesight recovered.

I didn't escape illness and often got sick. I had diarrhoea and tapeworms and lost a lot of weight. To get rid of the worms I had to drink a very bitter juice which came from the same wild fruits we used to dye our clothes with. Grandmother had my uncle climb a tree and pick the fruit. She then combined the bitter liquid with coconut juice so it was easier to drink. The juice poisoned the worms. Grandmother had a recipe for diarrhoea as well. She would find a guava tree (they were everywhere) and take some slices of the bark and leaves. She'd simmer them with three cups of water until it reduced to a single cup, which I then had to drink. This was also bitter and we had no palm sugar to sweeten it like we used to, however it worked and was certainly better than rabbit poo! All the traditional remedies were so bitter I always started crying, refusing to drink them. Grandmother had to force them down my throat, and every sip I took made me shiver in disgust.

I survived my illnesses with the help of the local medicines, but malaria was by far the worst. Our village was surrounded by ponds, swamps and the paddy fields, all breeding grounds for mosquitoes, especially during the rainy season. We burned a fire in front of the house, loading it with damp hay and fresh bush vines to make it very smoky. The male adults would roll up their tobacco and smoke non-stop during their evening conversation. This kept the mozzies away, but somehow, I still caught malaria. Mosquitoes also carried yellow fever and dengue fevers, so perhaps I was lucky I only caught malaria - as bad as it was.

    I was hit by a high temperature at first followed by feeling so cold that, no matter how many blankets I wrapped myself under, I shivered uncontrollably. Then I would sweat just as badly, my temperature spiking again. I felt like I was on fire. Grandmother tended to me, putting a wet scarf between my teeth so I didn't bite my tongue. The village treatment was to rub coconut oil on my back. Although the oil smelled good, the rubbing was extremely painful. This was because she had a special way of doing it. Grandmother's most precious possession was a coin, so old its edges were worn smooth. She carried it with her everywhere in her shirt pocket. She would dip it into the oil, then press down hard with it, running it down my back and over my ribs. She used so much force the path of each stroke turned my back dark red - it felt like she was about to peel my skin off! They had to hold me down while she did it as I kicked and twisted and struggled desperately to get away from the pain. My only consolation was the bowl of coconut water I was given to drink once the treatment had ended - although this had a couple of earthworms swimming in it! They were there to bring down my fever. Each time I had my temperature she gave me the same treatment. When we ran out of oil she used water. The bruises were visible for weeks.

    I recovered. But Malaria never truly leaves your body. However, I didn't-ever have it as bad again. I don't know how it worked, but that ancient folk remedy kept me alive, despite my weak condition from the hunger, despite the severity of the pain, despite the fevers.

    Once the decision to open the communal kitchen was made, the Khmer Rouge went to each house confiscating any pots, pans, bowls, fry-pans, and plates they could find. Not one tin cup remained at home for drinking water; instead we had to use a coconut shell. All that was left were a couple of spoons and some buckets we used to carry water from the well. These spoons were important, we had to bring them to the communal kitchen with us. All our meals were prepared in the kitchen and all our eating was done there. They called us to eat with a gong made from an old truck wheel.

We weren't allowed to keep any food at home - nothing. And as well as the cooking utensils they carried away with them, they also confiscated a lot of other things. We were only left with some clothing, blankets and water barrels - and that was about it. Everything else became communal property. Chickens, ducks or pigs were taken to the communal farms. I was just glad they didn't take Lily.

Anyone caught cooking, or stealing from the communal vegetable garden, or taking bananas or coconuts would be punished accordingly. And we all knew what that meant: *Korsang*.

And to add to the agony, as if we had not already been robbed of everything else, there was something else they were about to remove from our family. One afternoon I arrived home from grazing my grandfather's oxen in the rice paddies to find the chief and an Angkar *Mett*, called Chum, at our new house. They had come for me as I now had an important role to play in our great new society. All the boys and girls between ten and fifteen were being sent to labour camps.

It soon transpired that it was not only me who would be taken. Even five-year-old kids were being sent to live together in their own camps. My younger brother, Huang and Chong were taken and only Hun, still a toddler, was left behind. It was our parent's worst nightmare, but they could not show resentment. *Mett* Chum tried to comfort our parents, promising them that Angkar would take good care of us - that in fact we would be treated better than if we had been at home.

"*Mett*, there is nothing to worry about. Angkar will look after *Mett's* children. Angkar will feed them. There will be no shortage of anything. Angkar will take care of them better than *Mett* can. *Mett* must trust Angkar. *Mett's* children are now Angkar's children of the frontier."

Angkar said we had not yet been corrupted by the world, and we were young enough to learn Angkar's way. We were to be the eyes and ears of Angkar. We were to be the foot soldiers and the future. We were the "Children of the Frontier."

The Khmer Rouge and their Angkar had taken away everything; we went from zero to nothing. We had not much left to give besides our lives.

As I was led away by Chum to join the other boys, I was already afraid and lonely. I had now learned to suppress my emotions, understanding that it was dangerous to show dismay or sadness. Unlike my first day of school in Phnom Penh, this time I did not cry.

Chapter Eight

Boys Labour Camp

It was another evening at the camp, and our camp leader was brainwashing us again, pacing back and forth in front of us and shouting.

"*Mett* shall all be grateful to Angkar! There is only one Angkar in this new regime! Angkar feeds *Mett*. Angkar is all things to all *Mett*. *Mett* must dedicate themselves to Angkar. Comrades are Angkar's children of the frontier!"

The camp was little over a kilometre from our village, but I was not allowed to visit my parents and stay with them overnight. I had never been separated from them before, the longest time I had been away from home was a day at school. I remembered my parents' haunted eyes as I was led away, and knew they were naturally worried about me.

"What is Angkar going to do with my little boys?"

Our camp was bleak. There were no girls, as they had a camp of their own. Most of the boys were around my age, some a few years older. Many had already been there for a while. Our accommodation was an old long hut. The walls were made of palm leaves and the roof was thatched straw. It had a floor of split bamboo about half a metre above the ground where we all slept there together, and a central walkway. Not far from the hut was a small pond, which we used for washing and sometimes swimming. It was also where we got our drinking water. We were given two meals a day - lunch and dinner - and this offered us some comfort as we ate at the village communal kitchen, so sometimes we caught glimpses of our families. Each of us would be given a small bowl of rice and some soup, which had been made with some tiny pieces of meat and vegetables like morning glory, watercress, young palm fruits or banana tree.

We were divided into small groups with some older local boys selected as the leader of each group. Mine was a teenager called Pang, probably about fourteen. I had known him and his elderly mother back at the village, which is why I remember his name. I cannot recall many of the other boys' names because we all had to address each other as *Mett*. We were just faces without names.

The supervisor wore a pair of tight blue shorts and a neat polo shirt. He did not get involved in heavy or dirty work like we were forced to do, he just gave orders. He was also our Khmer instructor - possibly he was an ex-school teacher. Khmer lessons were given to the younger boys in the morning before we started work. There were no books or pencils. We sat on the ground listening and watching him write on a small board. He showed us the alphabet, and within a couple of months I could read and write in Khmer.

The teacher appeared well educated and intelligent. Our lessons began to branch out. One day he started talking about geography. I remember the class well. He asked us whether the earth was flat, oval or round. It was an intriguing question I was surprised to be asked, given our situation. Then, one day not long afterwards, he disappeared and all lessons stopped. Permanently.

There were a few men from the village who also stayed at the camp, local carpenters and farmers who taught us how to build with local materials, and to make bamboo baskets and cart wheels. We made all our own tools, smelting iron at the workshop and forming it into sickles and knives.

It was time for us to learn about agricultural work. Rice planting occurred in two stages. The first was when the whole crop was sown. This had happened just before the start of the monsoon by Old People using oxen to draw a plough. The earth had been turned over, loosening the soil and uprooting weeds. It took both skill and strength to manoeuvre a plough and the stubborn oxen, so even Angkar knew this was best left to farmers with years of experience. It would have been pointless to let the New People try. The paddies were filled with water to give the ground a good soak. Then women, riding a flat plough facing backwards, pushed rice grains into the saturated mud. If there was too much water the seeds would float and be eaten by birds. Too little water and the rice plants would shrivel and die. Planting had happened a month previously and the seedlings were now nearly 30 centimetres high and it was time to thin them out, with the thinnings transplanted into other fields.

Being from the city, I had never worked in a paddy field before. On that first day, because of my light complexion, I found myself the target of teasing and bullying. The other kids threw mud at me and pushed me around, saying, "Black people are heaven's children, but you're white like a Chinese willy!" It was true, I was paler than most Khmer boys. I had spent too much time inside - even the ethnic Chinese kids from the village, used to an outdoors life, were darker than me. Until now, even if I was outside I kept my shirt on. It only came off when I had a bath. Under the new regime - in a world where we were supposed to be equal - dark skin was considered superior to white. I did the only sensible thing I could think of: I took off my shirt and covered myself with mud.

Mama happened to pass the field and told me to put my shirt back on because of sunburn, but it was too late. The next day I was badly burned and of course there was nothing available to soothe it. I had to sleep lying on my front for a couple of nights. As the rice transplanting season continued over the next couple of months, however, I gradually became darker.

Once we were finished with the rice we were given other tasks. My job was to look after the ducks. Each morning I let them out of the barn and took them to a paddy field to swim. The monsoon season was well underway by now, the paddies were green with young rice plants. There was lots of water for the ducks. I just had to make sure they didn't go too far away, or do too much damage to the rice as they dug for insects and worms among the plants. While doing this, they left their droppings behind, which made good fertiliser. Compared to what some of the other kids had to do, my job was light work. All I had to do was feed them rice bran twice a day and make sure they were happy. They had a better life than me!

Every morning, I woke up earlier than everyone else so I could collect their eggs and take them to the kitchen. The barn had a low ceiling, about a metre high. It was dark and smelled of duck poo. I had to squat to walk, being careful not to disturb them. If they became too frightened they would run around and damage the eggs. Before I went to the kitchen I had to show the eggs to the camp supervisor for inspection. He would question me if there was one egg less than the previous day. If the number went up it was fine, but if there was one perceived egg missing I would be in trouble.

"Why is there one egg less than yesterday?"

I couldn't tell him. Some ducks just didn't lay eggs every day. The barn was close to our hut, sometimes at night I heard them quacking and rushing around their barn in fear. I suppose I should have gone to investigate, but I was too scared to be outside at night. Some ducks laid outside the barn in the daytime, so that occasionally we'd come across eggs in the mud or in the grass at the side of the fields. If we found an egg like this, it was a treasure and we kept it, although it was not allowed of course.

After a few weeks, I learnt how to cheat the system. Once I worked out how many eggs were expected, I would stash surplus eggs away and cover them with hay. I would come back later in the day on the pretence of preparing the barn for the ducks' return, and would collect the eggs to take to my grandparents. I would roll up one leg of my trousers and carefully place the eggs inside it. It was a very dangerous thing to do because if someone took a closer look, they would notice that one of my trouser legs was shorter than the other. My grandmother later sewed a secret pocket inside my shorts, just large enough to fit in a couple of eggs. It was dangerous for her too - if she was seen with contraband food she would be in as much trouble as me. She had to make sure there was no trace of the eggshells. To do this - and to cook the egg - she would wrap it in clay and put it on the fire. Once it was ready she would peel off the clay, which had now bonded to the shell.

The clay (along with the shell) was ground into fine dust and spread amongst the ash. It was a lengthy process to cook just one egg, but necessary because if we had been caught it might have been fatal. Mama told me not to steal eggs, worried about the consequences for both me and the rest of the family.

I kept doing it for a while. Then, one morning, I went back into the barn as usual to collect a couple of eggs I had hidden earlier. I had put one into the secret pocket and was standing there arranging my shorts so it didn't look like I had an egg hanging between my legs, when I looked up to see Pang standing in front of me. My heart started racing and I could feel the blood rushing through my veins. I knew I was in trouble, maybe big trouble. Would he give me extra work, or keep me hungry for a day - or was this my death sentence? I stammered my rehearsed excuse.

"I found these eggs just now. The ducks must have laid them after I did my morning collection."

Pang must have known from the look on my face that I was lying, but he chose to be kind, and told me I could keep them. Despite the risks, I was just too hungry to stop stealing the eggs.

Life continued in our new way, and next season Angkar rotated my duck patrolling work to a younger child and my next assignment was to work in the vegetable garden with a small group of other boys. There were a few gardens like it in the village, and this one was about the size of a football field. There were some elderly ladies, like my grandmother, working there too, and they taught us the basic rules of gardening. Grandma showed me which plants were weeds, how to dig rows for planting and how to sow seeds. We grew eggplants, tomatoes and cucumbers, along with beans, pumpkins, melons and other Cambodian vegetables. Once they were ready for harvest, we had to prepare for the next crop. We'd clear the old plants and let the soil lie fallow for a few days, before fertilising it. After this it was time for planting. Grandma taught me an important gardening rule: "Plant in the evening for leaves, plant in the morning for fruits." So, lettuces or vegetables such as Pak Choy would be planted in the late afternoon, tomatoes and eggplants in the morning. I don't know whether there was a scientific basis for this, but it seemed to work well.

Looking after the vegetable garden was harder than caring for the ducks. There were four of us assigned to it and we had to water it a couple of times a day. It was important work, as we were feeding the village so we weren't given many opportunities for a break. I, who had never carried anything heavier than my school bag, now spent my day lugging two buckets full of water. They weighed around ten kilos each, and I wobbled around from the creek to the field with a yoke across my shoulders. Sometimes I carried those buckets all day. We watered morning, afternoon and evening. The heavy yoke rubbed against my shoulders and made them very sore. I had blisters, but I had to keep working, pain or no pain. Sometimes I would not fill the buckets to the top to make them lighter, but this meant I had to make more trips. More trips meant more pain. Eventually my shoulders would grow numb, although they would be even sorer later. I knew not to complain about the pain.

If we weren't watering, we were fertilizing. Every morning after the cows and oxen left the barn we'd have to collect the manure and take it to the garden, mixing it with leaves and dirt to enrich it further. It was used for both the vegetables and the rice paddies.

We also had to collect the waste from the outdoor toilets. This was much worse than collecting cow manure. The toilets were holes in the ground less than a metre deep. Some toilets did not even have a hole because they were elevated above ground. There were a couple of logs to squat on surrounded by four low walls made from palm leaves - just the bare minimum height to keep you concealed while you were using them.

I had a shovel and the buckets I used to transport water. Because it had been dry the crap usually had a hard crust, but underneath it was still wet and as bad as you can imagine. It was full of maggots and reminded me of the body I had seen in the fields. That first day was the worst, and I had goose bumps all over and was constantly gagging. I knew not to complain. I transferred the waste into large barrels, adding water, letting the mixture sit for a few days before using it as fertilizer. The smell was unbearable. No matter how much water I added, the shit still smelled like shit. After a while, though, I became more tolerant to it and was able to put my bare hands into the barrels to clean them out. To get the work done faster I would scoop out the faeces with my fingers. I had maggots crawling up my arms but it didn't worry me anymore.

Because of the fertilizer and the watering, we had a very productive garden. Like with the ducks, though, we weren't supposed to eat anything that wasn't provided by the communal kitchen. We were always hungry, however, and surrounded by delicious things like tomatoes and cucumbers. I knew that if I was caught picking them there would be consequences. I might be beaten, or forced to do extra work. One day the temptation was too strong. I squatted down in the field as low as possible, hiding between the vines. I was terrified, but I was starving. The next day, one of the leaders inspected the garden. He called us over to interrogate us, "Why is there one cucumber missing?!"

Everyone else looked puzzled, but I had butterflies and the first twinges of panic. It was inconceivable they kept track of every cucumber! There were a few nervous responses, "I'm not sure. I don't know. Didn't we pick that one yesterday?"

No one knew that I had eaten it. If it had been another boy, I wouldn't have known either. When it came to Angkar, I didn't trust any of the other kids, and they didn't trust me. No one stuck their neck out. Some boys curried favour with the leaders by acting as unofficial spies.

The leader was looking at us, still trying to determine the culprit. It turned out that he counted the vegetables, going through the crops as soon as each day's harvest was completed. How could I have been so dumb and eaten one in such an obvious position? Luckily, I had dropped a few small pieces of the cucumber on the ground nearby, and in the end, they decided that a rat had done it. I had been very fortunate. I would not try the same thing again - I couldn't rely on luck a second time. It was just too dangerous.

I only worked in the vegetable garden for one season, and then it became the responsibility of the younger kids including Chong. Unfortunately, he soon found himself in trouble when he was accused of stealing a melon. His team leader and the other local Khmer boys beat him severely, and nearly drowned him by putting his head inside a jar full of water. He never fully recovered, and afterwards suffered from terrible migraine headaches. And he didn't steal the melon. He had seen an old man walking past the field. The man had told him he was hungry, and could he have some fruit? My brother was just five and didn't know any better, and he let the man pick a melon. Maybe the old man was greedy, because he picked one of the biggest in the field, one whose absence was very noticeable. Just like the cucumbers, the Khmer Rouge leader counted everything.

On the direction of Angkar the older boys were sent to help with the grain harvest. The fields were full of golden brown rice plants surrounded by tall, slender sugar palms in all directions. Despite the presence of the Khmer Rouge, it was a beautiful sight. The view was amazing - and so was the smell. Just walking to the crops made my stomach rumble. Finally, I thought, we would have rice again! The seed heads were so heavy that the old, fragile stems could barely keep them off the ground.

This was my first experience of the rice harvest. We started in early December, and kept working through till February. I was instructed in the use of a Khmer rice sickle, a curved blade with a wooden handle. Its sharp blade mowed through the rice. Once I had cut enough I would gather up the fallen stems and tie them into bundles, laying them in a straight line ready to be taken to the village.

The local boys and farmers who knew their way around the fields had the job of driving the ox carts which would pick up our rice and take it to the village to be threshed and milled.

Sometimes the New People were made to carry it to the village using the yoke I had come to hate so much when watering the vegetable garden. Once we got there it didn't end, because we were made to thresh our rice in the heat of the day. Once threshed, the grain was taken to one of the rice stores, while the hay was put aside to be used as roofing or cattle food.

Once the harvest was finished, Angkar sent us to work on the irrigation system. We were not given an opportunity to rest. We had to start digging channels in preparation for the monsoon. The vegetable garden had been bad, the harvest had been worse, but this was even harder.

My day started when a bell rang to get us out of bed at the break of dawn. I had a daily quota to dig: a ditch two metres long by a metre wide, half a metre deep. As we did not have a proper measuring device every morning our team leader would pick a straight stick from the bush, cut it to approximately a metre long and we used this to measure our quota. We soon became very familiar with how long a metre was. This was a lot of soil to carry onto the top of the banks. We used hoes to scrape soil into two baskets. We would then lift them by use of the yoke, and stagger up the bank under the weight. Like robots we stopped when another bell rang at lunchtime. Another bell would tell us to return to work, another near sunset told us we could stop for the day. We could only pack up our gear and line up at the communal kitchen for dinner if we'd met our quota. We didn't need another bell to tell us it was time for bed - we were so exhausted that having a quick wash before lying down on our bamboo beds was all we could think about - until the next morning when the roosters started crowing and the damn bell rang again.

This was our routine now, our new way of life. The roosters would wake us, the bell would tell us to get up. We would stumble around, half asleep, finding our baskets, yokes and hoes. We would stumble along the road to our workplaces. No one had a watch anymore, we learned to tell the time by the length of our shadows. About ten o'clock, it was a metre to the left of me, at 2pm it was a metre to the right. I knew it was midday when I stood right on top of it, although I had another way of knowing it was noon - the thunder in my stomach telling me how hungry I was!

As I grew older my workload started to increase - and I was more frequently bullied. It had been easier when I looked after the ducks, as I had been alone. In the vegetable garden, we had worked in small groups, often by ourselves in our assigned areas. Now I was surrounded by the local boys, all eager to tease me because I was Chinese, or because I was a New Person. It became really ugly at times, and my only desire was to stay away from trouble and survive until bedtime.

The thing I hated the most was when they tormented me because of my father's voice.

"*Eeer, ooor,* your father sounds like a cow!"

One day, while digging the canal for water irrigation with the rest of the boys, I couldn't stand it any longer. The boy in question was a Khmer, a New Person from Phnom Penh. His father had been a kick boxer, a sport known for its high rate of fatalities. It was so violent it was rumoured they kept an empty coffin by the ringside during every match. Back in the city I had enjoyed seeing movies with Shaolin monks demonstrating their martial arts ability. Maybe I had talked about them, because this kid wanted to see if I knew any Kung Fu. Presumably he was going to see how I stacked up against his kick boxing. I had never learned to fight. He teased me further, asking if I knew Bruce Lee. No, I didn't know Bruce Lee. The closest I had come to him was watching "The Big Boss" and having a black and white postcard of him showing his famous flying kick. I had often climbed onto my parent's bed to imitate it, without success, it should be said. I had even practised his three kicks in one signature move. Now I was about to put all this "training" into practice.

The sun was sitting low and red in the west after a long hot day. All I could think of was finishing work, but this boy was clearly spoiling for a fight. I tried to avoid confrontations if I could, as usually my tormentors were bigger, local kids. This boy was about my size. I had had one fight back in Phnom

Penh with my cousin, Hong, and I had come out on top in that one, so I figured I had a chance. I was tired though, so I still tried to avoid it. I walked away, but he followed me and wrestled me to the ground, and we rolled down into one of the channels we'd been digging. He pinned my arms and sat on my stomach, leaning his face over mine, preparing to spit.

All the other boys were watching us, no doubt expecting me to get badly beaten as this kid had been in a lot of fights before. Instead of struggling I relaxed, moving my head from side to side to avoid the long strand of saliva that now dangled from his mouth. I took the opportunity to calm right down and regain my breath. As soon as I could I flipped him off with my hips and then stood up, keeping my distance. I knew I wasn't strong enough to hold him down and that it was important not to get too close in case he tried to pin me again. He got off the ground and faced me, ready to take me down. All the boys, and even our team leader, had their eyes glued on us. They preferred watching a fight to stopping one. He punched with his right hand, missing me, and I let him have it, a punch to his right eye, another to his left temple, and a combination to his head. It didn't take many more punches until he dropped to the ground. I didn't let up. It was my turn to sit on him, but I didn't worry about spitting. I punched away until his nose started bleeding, then calmly stood up and went to continue my work. I still had my quota to fill and I didn't want to miss out on dinner. He lay on the ground for a while longer, and when he stood up he started staggering towards the forest until someone guided him back to the path. Like me, he had to finish his quota.

He shook my hand and apologised the next day, and we developed a friendship. His name was Ah-Thy, but I don't know what happened to him - he disappeared after the next dry season.

On another occasion, I was randomly assigned to look after a herd of cows with a local Khmer kid who knew how to lead the oxen as we were walking along the paddy banks. He had a gentle command of them and could tie them securely, even wash them. I was the opposite. I would lead the oxen with one in front and one behind, but they would never walk straight for me, and wander all over the place. I struggled and they ran. When I concentrated on the one in front, the one at the back got into the paddy fields and started eating the rice plants - or sometimes it was the other way around. Washing them terrified me. It was hard enough to get them into the water, but once there it was easy to get knocked down by a kick from a hind leg. I had to hold the leash very firmly so they kept their heads still and didn't spear me with a horn. They weren't aggressive, but were easily startled by a sudden movement. There were a couple of times they shook their huge heads unexpectedly and bruised me in the thigh and ribs with the end of their horns - scary stuff for a city kid like me!

Although he was younger than me the other kid was bigger and fatter, and I called him "Fat Boy." I wondered how he could be so healthy when so many of us barely had enough food to survive.

One hot day when we were out looking after the oxen, the sun high overhead, we decided to have a swim. We tied up the cows and found a small pond. I didn't know how to swim at that time, so I would stay at the edge of any bodies of water, or find a log to hang onto. Fat Boy could swim well. He said there was a log at the bottom of the water, just a metre down. If I stood on it my head would be above the water. I balanced on the log, but he was either deliberately mean or perhaps didn't realise I couldn't swim, because he started to rock the log for fun, and threw me off balance. I struggled to find a tree root to hang onto, kicking and struggling to keep myself afloat. Eventually I found a vine and got out of the pond safely, but not before I'd taken a few mouthfuls of dirty water.

I was angry - he had nearly killed me, and although he was bigger than me I went for him. My usual technique was to finish my opponent as quickly as possible because I didn't have the stamina for a long fight. I went straight for his eyes, and he was soon seeing stars. He ran off quickly, although a few days later he came back to challenge me again - the result for round two was the same as for round one.

Maybe we should have felt more compassion for each other, seeing we faced a common enemy, but we were kids under enormous pressure, and we didn't always react appropriately. As a result, there were many fights, and harassment and bullying were common, and every fight you won provoked new challengers.

Not long after the kid with the oxen I learned how to swim - or at least how to stay afloat. At the beginning of our second monsoon season I was relaxing in the pond in the middle of the camp which was quite full after the recent rainfall. A boy named Hak who used to live over the road from my grandparents, started taunting me, obviously looking for a fight.

There were adults nearby also swimming, and some further off in the kitchen and woodwork shop watching, but none of them did anything to intervene. Hak was bigger than me, and at least a head taller.

He teased me about my father's voice, and every now and then he deliberately jumped over my head into the pond. In Cambodia, we believe that the space just above the head is sacred because we have our guardian angel hovering there. For this reason, we never walked between people's legs or passed underneath clothes lines. Hak also knew that I wasn't a strong swimmer and he kept trying to pull the banana log I was using as a float away from me.

I left the pond to get away from him, but he came after me, now being very aggressive. I was ready to fight him, but was worried because he was so much larger. He started pushing and kicking, and I had no choice but to defend myself. We were standing near the edge of the pond, facing each other. He hit me, once, twice, quickly, and I was stunned. Another combination, one two. And another. I ducked and weaved, waiting for an opportunity to fight back, but he was too tall and my punches weren't reaching him. Then he went for a kick to the side of my head, but I ducked underneath it so he missed me by a hair, and then he slipped heavily on the muddy bank. This was the chance I needed. I was able to punch him in the face and he fell right back into the pond, and that was the end of the fight. He half challenged me again a couple of times after that, but had grown wary of me so I didn't have to take him seriously. I didn't want to have another fight with him because I knew I had been lucky. If his kick had landed it would have been a very different story.

I realised I had become, for now at least, a survivor. I had made a few friends. I had stolen a few eggs and been caught red handed yet had not been punished. I had stolen a cucumber from under Angkar's nose, and had won the fights I had been in - and not had to face the wrath of Angkar for them, either. The boys no longer picked on me. I liked to think it was because of those few knockouts, but I knew in my heart it wasn't only that. Our living conditions were getting worse, and no one had the time or energy for fighting anymore. The long hours of hard labour were taking their toll on even the most dedicated bullies.

As well as the hard labour, our food ration was shrinking. Initially Angkar gave us properly cooked rice, but very soon it became rice porridge. Angkar explained that Kor had to become self-reliant. Whatever was produced in the village had to be used in the village. Because last year's stores were growing low we had to live on what remained until the next harvest - and that meant rice porridge until the following year.

My body was growing and I was constantly hungry, so whenever I had any free time - which wasn't very often - I would forage for food in the bush. This had one advantage I hadn't foreseen. By the end of the first dry season, the local boys in camp forgot my status as New People because I now looked as dirty as one of them. I had been wearing the same set of clothing since I had arrived. My pale complexion was as dark as theirs. My hair was messy and full of lice. Sometimes I scratched frantically like a dog with fleas. Back in the old days Mama had removed any lice with a fine comb, in the new world I had to cover my head with mud and let it dry. Afterwards I would rinse it off, and the lice would be washed away with the mud.

We were given a new team leader, another local Khmer boy of fourteen who was kind and reasonable. Although he worked us hard, he also let us hunt together. Sometimes when we were clearing the bush or digging irrigation channels we would see a rat or a snake. We'd get very excited and start chasing. Not one of these poor animals escaped the Children of the Frontier. One day we chased a cobra across a field. One kid poked at its head while another crept up behind it and grabbed it by the tail. This boy's name was Rotthyna, but sometimes he was teased and called *Rottouna* (where do you run to?). He didn't run from anything, though, even cobras. He swung the snake's head as hard as he could onto the ground, killing it instantly. That's what I call brave, catching and killing a cobra bare handed. There was another snake that was supposed to be even more poisonous than a cobra. Its local name translates as the "black buffalo." The story went that a man bitten by a cobra could run across a couple of rice fields before the venom took effect, but with a black buffalo he would be lucky to make it across just one. Those of us who had been afraid of snakes mostly lost our fear: our hunger was stronger than snake's venom.

Another natural food source was honey. The desire to put something in our stomachs was stronger than the pain from a few bee stings. I would smoke the bees even in the tallest trees, and come down the tree with as much honeycomb as I could carry. I set up bird traps, and wandered from one sugar palm to the next looking for fruit.

I had drunk sugar palm juice and eaten the soft sugar palm seeds in Phnom Penh, but I had never seen a sugar palm tree. Out here in the village, however, they were everywhere. Only the female trees bore fruit, the males produced the sap we used to make palm sugar. They were tapped like a maple tree, with a cylinder attached to them high up to collect the watery sweet syrup. Sugar palms became the major source of nutrition for my growing body. Knowing how to climb one of these trees without a ladder was essential.

The main thing you needed was a rope which you tied into a loose ring around the trunk. You would hook this around your ankles. Then you'd wrap your arms around the tree, pressing your body against the trunk. You'd reach up, then drag up your feet. Then you'd put pressure on the rope so you could stand up again and repeat the process. You'd use the rope the same way to come down, employing it as a brake so you didn't slip and slide down too quickly. Sugar palms were generally tall, sometimes up to fifteen metres high. If you made a single mistake you could end up flat on your back on the hard floor of a dry, cracked rice field. There were no safety nets.

The next thing you needed was a sharp axe, not too heavy, but large enough to cut down the fruit with one hand while using the other to hang onto the tree. Like the other kids, I had a little axe which I carried all the time tucked into the waistband of my shorts. We'd use our axes to cut tree branches and vines or chop up snakes, rats, frogs or fish.

Once up a tree, you had to be careful not to drop your axe. The last thing you wanted was to see it fall to the ground after you had struggled up the trunk and then through the branches towards a particularly large, juicy fruit. Sometimes I only had the energy for one climb - if I dropped the axe that was it.

Because we were all hungry all the time, seeing a sugar palm with a lot of fruit was a good feeling. Of course, all the low and easy to climb trees near the village were long empty - it was only the tall ones some distance away that still had fruit on them.

Rotthyna was one of the best climbers. I used to watch him, wanting to be like him. He had dark olive skin and like the rest of us wore torn black shirt and trousers, a red *Krama* and an axe tucked into his waistband. He was a natural at everything: catching cobras with his bare hands and killing rats on the run with his slingshot. He could smoke beehives and climb up and down sugar palms without needing a rope. Sometimes he would raid the sugar juice cylinders, and share his bounty with us. The boys relied on him to do the hard work, and we loved him and he loved us in return. There was one sugar palm that no one dared climb. All season it taunted us with its juicy, inaccessible fruit sitting above the fat hump near the top. The boys said it had a hump because it was pregnant. Rotthyna made it to the top, but while trying to reach for the fruit he slipped and fell to the ground, and his axe ended up embedded in his back. It was very sad. He wasn't the first to die like this, but because he was the best climber and so well loved, his death was a great loss to our team at the boys' camp. Sadly, I was to become too used to my friends dying far too young.

CHAPTER NINE

THE MEETING

Following our Khmer custom of hope and prayer that we would have a good harvest and the village chief allowed us to celebrate our traditional rice festival at the beginning of our first harvest of the year. This was normally a popular event across rural Cambodia as it marked the beginning of the new season. In the old days, the farmers made rice crackers by harvesting some rice before it was fully ripe, when it was still milky and unformed. They would roast it in a hot clay pot until it turned light brown and started to jump around, just like popcorn. The smell was amazing. Then they'd pour it onto a mill, where it would be crushed and flattened with a wooden pole to make it small enough to be formed into crackers.

"You can have as much as you like. Eat until you are satisfied," said the village chief. We ate to our heart's content, but Grandfather Huot warned everyone, "Be careful, don't eat too much. You'll be suffocated when the rice expands."

These rice crackers at the festival smell and tasted wonderful. They were not our usual food, but were savouries. Everyone at the village enjoyed this luxury, some for the first time. Sadly, for some of the New People, it would their last time as well. Some New People ate more than their stomachs could handle. Whether they really died of internal suffocation from having too much or by some other means, nobody will ever know. Throughout our first rainy season under Angkar, the purge had already begun. Every day, we saw families trucked away by Angkar allegedly taking them for *Korsang* - but we never saw them again. They would take two or three families at once, sometimes up to twenty people, but no one dared look, let alone keep track. We were all scared that watching too attentively would draw attention to ourselves and lead to us being next on the trucks.

They would call families to attend a private *Anprachum*

"meeting" and then these people would disappear. The Khmer Rouge looked for any excuse to cleanse the New People to create a one-mind society. We began to realise they were being killed in huge numbers. The Khmer Rouge began rounding up those New People with a connection to the army or previous Lon Nol government, anyone who had been to school or taught in one, religious people, merchants, anyone with a foreign connection was at risk. Being a wealthy Chinese from Phnom Penh was enough to be designated an enemy of Angkar: in other words, enemy of the old people. People who were not farmers or peasants were considered capitalists of the Old Society. The Khmer Rouge *Yothea* started to refer to the New People as bourgeois, adding that "The only good bourgeois is a dead bourgeois." They literally used the French word "*bourgeois*" of which I had no clue then and I am quite sure that they, themselves, had no idea what that word meant either. They would throw this taunt at us if we were slow in the rice fields or when digging the channels.

A new expression began to be heard in the village, "Comrade is of no use to Angkar and there is neither gain to keep nor loss to kill". It wasn't enough that starvation and disease were decimating us, the Khmer Rouge were doing it as well. Because they were so brainwashed the young Khmer Rouge *Yothea* embraced the mantra wholeheartedly, "there is no gain to keep nor loss to kill." They acted as if they would obtain some kind of bonus by identifying, capturing and eliminating enemies of Angkar. Their hearts were full of hatred. They despised anyone from the city. They were the children of poor uneducated peasants who had been put in a position of total power over anyone they perceived as having superior status. They told us that the bourgeois from the city had oppressed the farmers and peasants for decades by stealing from them the fruits of their sweat and blood for profit. Now it was time for revenge.

Some fortunate families like ours had learned early the consequences of honesty when it came to family history, so we had escaped their attention and they believed our story of having been a poor family struggling to make a living in the harsh city. As the purges continued; however, and as they kept killing anyone they thought of as elite, they started to run out of people to execute. Their attention turned towards people with a link to ethnic minority groups: Vietnamese was first, then Chinese and Muslims. So far, my family had been lucky enough to escape "the meeting", but sadly our luck was about to run out.

I became their first target. The leader of Children of the Frontier, *Mett* Churn, thought that I was Vietnamese because of my light complexion; that Mama was protecting my true identity. He started saying I would be sent away for "the meeting" with some other Vietnamese families who had come to settle in the village. *Mett* Churn summoned my mother to clarify my identity.

Naturally Mama defended me vigorously.

"I am one of the local villagers and the boy is my son. Comrade can ask the chief, he has known me since I was a girl and he's seen me bringing him to visit my parents since he was a little boy."

Somehow her pleas were listened to, and my life was spared. Not so for kids who really did have a Vietnamese background. They were deemed to be an enemy of Angkar and all enemies "were not a gain to keep nor a loss to kill."

Father, too, came very close to being called for the meeting on more than one occasion. The first time was when he was summoned by the chief for a private meeting where he was accused of being slow and lazy in the fields. Father had lived in the city all his life and had never set foot in a rice paddy before now. As hard as he tried, he could never keep up with farmers who had being working outdoors all their lives. Mama managed to convince the chief that Father would improve, he just needed time. My mother trusted her instincts, if she saw Father brought to a meeting she never failed to accompany him, whether she was invited or not.

Another time he was lighting a cigarette with a lighter he'd borrowed from the communal kitchen when he was accused of stealing it. (When we first arrived in the village, the Old People still had tobacco trees growing in their backyards. After Angkar prohibited the private growing of tobacco, Father used dry guava leaves instead.) He was asked about the lighter, but because of his speech impediment, which became worse when he was nervous, it was difficult to understand him. He didn't deal with confrontation at the best of times, and would usually walk out of an argument because he couldn't make himself understood. Once again it was Mama to the rescue, pointing out that Father had been lent the lighter by another communal kitchen worker, and that it would be returned. The man who had lent him the lighter backed up the story. Mama then had them search Father to prove he had no other contraband - like food.

If it was not for Mama, and because Grandfather Huot and the chief were Old People, Father would have been taken away long ago. Mama had her heart in her mouth every day, knowing she could lose him so easily, and could in fact lose any or all of us. Once one member of a New People family was convicted, a death sentence was lowered on the whole family.

They say lightening never strikes the same place twice, but it happened to Father three times. As the Khmer Rouge purges continued, Father's name was once again called. This time it was a case of mistaken identity. There were two other families in the village whose fathers had the same first name as my father. One lived opposite my grandfather's house and was a plumber, the other also lived not too far away from us. He was a doctor. Once again it came down to Mama and the chief. Fortunately, because of the times when she had graciously let the Khmer Rouge take away our bikes and Grandfather Huot's house, they believed she was faithful to Angkar and eventually they let Father go. The plumber who lived opposite my grandfather's house also survived but unfortunately the same cannot be said about the doctor and his family.

The family who lived next door to us weren't so lucky either. There were eight or nine of them, and they were all called for "the meeting". Their crime was due to their daughter's beauty. She was sixteen or seventeen - considered old enough to be married - and was quite stunning, especially when standing next to a local farm girl worn down by a hard life. Her family were Chinese from Phnom Penh and she had silky smooth, pale skin and big round eyes. It wasn't her fault that one of the boys fell for her. Angkar disagreed. No one was allowed to have a relationship without Angkar's consent.

"The boy must marry a local girl. Comrade cannot marry one of the New People."

The young man's request and Angkar's refusal went on for some time, until eventually the Khmer Rouge lost patience and sent the girl and her family away. At first it seemed that they were going to take the wannabe groom as well, but he was the only tinsmith in the village, and could make buckets, bowls and spoons, so he lived, and the girl and her whole family died, even the young children. This was Angkar's way, wiping out their entire bloodline just because they were New People. We lived with the primal fear of losing our entire family every day. It kept the New People silent and we hardly spoke to each other anymore.

It wasn't an accident that entire families were called, because along with wiping out genetics, it also ensured that no witnesses to the disappearances were left behind. Those of us with any brains knew that being called to *Anprachum Korsang* (meeting for re-education) meant we would be taken away and killed. One of our neighbours, a man named Boo Seng (Uncle Seng), told Mama that clothes were stripped from the victims and returned to the village to be re-distributed. "Look around, you'll see people wearing the clothes of those who have been taken away."

Mama lost a cousin to Angkar that first year for no reason.

"Sister, did you get a call to go to an *Anprachum* like my family?"

Mama shook her head. Both women became worried. Mama's cousin had a son about my age in the boys' camp with me. Angkar sent for him to be picked up and brought to the village. While this was happening, Mama ran for the chief. She begged him to spare the boy, saying she would adopt him and raise him as her own. The chief would not let her.

"If I don't obey Angkar, then my life, and that of my family, will be in the same position as your cousin."

So, two grandparents, two parents and one young boy were taken away for "the meeting" and never seen alive again. No one spoke up against it, for to do so would be to condemn yourself and your whole family. We were all in the same nightmare, from the chief down.

One by one the sons of the New People in the boys' camp disappeared. We knew they were dead. No one asked any questions, but we all knew the answer. We heard no evil, saw no evil and spoke no evil. It was better not to know. I put my head down and concentrated on my farming, on my digging, on my daily labour. I became a robot, knowing that the dumbest boy in the village had a greater chance of surviving this cruel, black hearted regimen than I did.

My beautiful, faithful dog, Lily, had nothing to do with the upper class, lower class or bourgeois; nothing to do with being a doctor or a farmer, she was just my pet. She had helped protect our trolleys on the long walk from the city, she had left her puppies for us and despite having no one to feed or care for her, she stayed at my grandparent's house. Since there was no cooking at home there was little chance of being offered scraps. There were no rations allocated for dogs. Occasionally she would follow my grandparents into the communal kitchen where she would be offered a few fish bones or crab shells. She was skinny and hardly had any flesh left on her. She was starving. One day my brother Huang caught a frog and gave it to Grandfather Huot. While he was chopping it up to eat, Lily was circling him, desperate for food. Grandfather Huot was hungry, too, he wasn't going to share. She kept coming closer and closer. Grandfather Huot picked up a piece of firewood, meaning to scare her, but he ended up whacking her on the nose. Lily was too weak and she collapsed. She died before the first anniversary of the regime. I must tell you that Grandfather Huot didn't waste what little meat there was on Lily, either, and she went straight into the pot. No one had pets anymore - Lily was the last dog in the village.

We almost lost Grandfather Huot during the first dry season, too. Although he had been fit enough to ride his bike all the way to Phnom Penh, under the regime he was skin and bone. He looked like a stick of bamboo. Once the camps started all his children were moved away, so there was no one to look after him. My parents were in a "mobile brigade" at a remote rice field. Even my grandmother had been sent away with a group of old women. One day Boo Seng (Uncle Seng) realised he hadn't seen Grandfather for a few days. This was unusual, Grandfather was normally very social. Boo Seng went inside his house and found him lying in a pool of diarrhoea. He gave my grandfather a wash and wanted to take him to the rudimentary hospital the Khmer Rouge had established, but my grandfather refused. He knew he would not be cured by a "doctor" of Angkar administering rabbit poo. Going to that hospital was the same as going to the graveyard. Boo Seng got word to Grandmother, who begged the Khmer Rouge to be allowed to care for him. Probably because of her age they showed leniency and she was given permission to return to the village. Like she had done for me, she took some of the bark of a guava tree, added it to three cups of water and simmered it down to one cup. Grandfather drank this and some coconut water to give him strength. Slowly and surely, miraculously, he began to recover.

CHAPTER TEN

BORROWED GRAVES

On the road from the village to the boys' camp the Khmer Rouge had built a jail. It sat by itself in the middle of a rice paddy surrounded by a fence of sticks. I would walk past it every time I went to the village or returned to the camp. I couldn't see inside because it was well covered, but I could hear people yelling and moaning, presumably being tortured. My heart would beat twice as fast when I heard them, and all I could do was put my head down and walk quickly. No one spoke about the prisoners or why they were in jail. We just didn't talk about it.

Occasionally we saw them in the fields, not close but near enough to see what they were doing - and how emaciated they were. They kept their eyes on the ground as they worked, looking for any kind of food. Their ears heard only two sounds. One was the voice of Angkar giving instructions, the other was the noise of a falling sugar palm fruit, the "para para, dok" it made as it hit leaves on its way to the ground. The prisoners would rush to the spot, scuffling over the fruit like hyenas, grabbing it and tearing it apart to get at the sweet juicy flesh.

Their skinny bodies inside their black pyjamas were much weaker and more fragile than ours. They looked like they had not eaten for months. They were given no privileges and were closely guarded by young Khmer Rouge *Yothea* with fierce hatred on their faces and in their hearts. We didn't understand how these young Khmer Rouge *Yothea* could have so much hate. They carried their AK47s ready to shoot at the first sign of escape. I dared not look at the prisoners for too long, and the prisoners kept their hollow eyes on the ground in their eternal search for food.

One day the boys and I were working in a creek to build a fish trap. We were going to catch fish, crab and shrimps - anything we could take back to the camp to cook. Because of our digging there was mud everywhere. A group of prisoners was marched near to us. One of them saw a small crab in the wet dirt. She quickly squatted down to pick it up and swallowed it in one go. Another saw a shrimp jumping in the mud and it, too, went straight into her mouth. Judging by their haggard and colourless faces, we knew the prisoners were living on even less food than we were - maybe just on one thin bowl of rice porridge a day.

One morning while working in the rice fields at the back of the village we found some skeletons lying on a low hill hidden in the bush. The local boys said they were the bones of former prisoners carried here by other prisoners and left to rot.

Late one afternoon, while grazing the oxen, I realised one had wandered off. I left the herd to Fat Boy and went looking for the escapee. I could hear the bell around its neck tinkling in the distance. Eventually I caught up to it on a small rise surrounded by thick bush. As I drew near I smelled something - the same smell I remembered from that rice paddy on the side of the road when we had come from Phnom Penh. It grew stronger as I came closer to it. I couldn't help myself: I was curious, I had to have a look. It was another small graveyard. There were now many of them scattered around us, hidden anywhere there was enough bush, but we were usually too afraid to go near them. The cattle liked them, though, because the grass was longer and the bushes were greener.

There was a dead body in a shallow grave, barely a metre long, probably only half a metre deep. One of its legs was sticking out of the ground. All around were other bones. The Khmer Rouge would make some people dig their own graves, however, because the ground was hard in the dry and sticky in the wet this was difficult to do. This victim had presumably disinterred the previous corpse, and at some time in the future he, too, would most likely be removed from the ground to make room for someone else. Who knows how many times one grave would be used? I pulled on the oxen's lead and walked quickly away from the terrible sight.

During the first dry season of Year Zero I had already

picked up some survival skills from the local boys. I had learnt how to hunt with a slingshot, how to catch a catfish with my bare hands, how to set a bird trap in the bush and most importantly how to be brave enough to climb palm trees. One skill I hadn't yet learned was how to produce palm juice. The sap of sugar palms is rich in calories and in normal times was made into palm sugar or fermented into an alcoholic drink: "sour palm water". These weren't normal times - all my starving body craved was the sweetness.

To tap the juice, you had to be a good climber and not be afraid of height, as you needed to get right to the top of the trees where the flowers were. Generally, the male flowers produced sweeter juice. The climbers would make long bamboo ladders and climb from tree to tree, using two sticks tied at one end to squeeze and massage the juice from the flowers. Once the flowers were ready they would cut their tips and hang them inside the hollow part of another long tube of bamboo. They would be left overnight while the sap dripped out of them, to be collected the next morning and often the following evening as well. The bamboo tubes were about half a metre long and could hold about two litres.

One day, back when I was looking after the ducks, I had watched one particular palm sapper with envy, knowing he would have taken a drink. One day I waited at the foot of a tree for him to come down, hoping he would offer me a taste. He let me sip from the fullest piece of bamboo, and we came to an arrangement. He would hide some of the cylinders of juice in the bush for me, and in return I would give him any duck eggs from the paddy. I had to squat behind a bush and be very careful not to let anyone see me drinking the juice. I always did this when the palm sapper was at the top of a tree, so that if I got caught he could not be blamed. The juice was very sweet and my body relished the sugar. I drank until I was full and my swollen stomach stuck out in contrast to my bony rib cage.

Palm trees were considered wild, and so it was permissible to get food from them. I knew Angkar wouldn't mind if I fell from a tree and killed myself, not when so many others were dying every day. I started looking for a tree of my own so I could have palm juice any time I wanted. It was well known that the tallest trees produced the sweetest sap, so I reasoned I would find a short one as there was more likelihood it had been left alone. Surely even short sugar palms would be better than no sugar? My friend the sap tapper helped me make a bamboo ladder, found some abandoned tools for me, and told me how to massage the flowers. He also showed me a tree that was no longer used. For him it was not worth climbing, but surely it would have enough sap in it for one small boy? It worked! It didn't produce much, but there was enough to keep me coming back for a couple of weeks.

That first sugar palm was short and leaned to one side and was perfect to practice on. Now I had the confidence to tap something taller. I found one behind some trees near the river. Five metres was about as high as I had been before, but this one was closer to ten. I fastened my bamboo ladders against the trunk, and climbed up. The hard part was to get to the end of the branches where the flowers were. It was difficult and painful. Palm trees have sharp spikes running along both sides of the stems. If you moved too quickly it was like being attacked by a botanical chainsaw, and I soon had cuts all over my arms and legs. I had to hold onto the ladder with one hand while stripping off the spikes with my small axe until I had cleared enough away to leap onto the top branches where the flowers were.

One hot afternoon I ran from my lunch break to collect some palm juice from my new tree. While I was high up in its branches I heard a sound: someone nearby was digging, using a hoe to try and split the hard, dry ground. I didn't pay it much attention initially as I was focussed on getting some juice, but peering down I realised one of the prisoners from the small jail was there. It was strange that there was only one prisoner; normally they were led around in groups. I stayed in the tree, watching. I realised that the prisoner was accompanied by some guards. Perhaps they were talking, but I was too far away to hear anything. They made him kneel in front of the grave he had dug. They took his *Krama* and tied his arms above the elbows so they were behind his back. One of the Khmer Rouge *Yothea* raised up the hoe. There was a loud clack as it came down on the prisoner's head, a sound like a coconut being struck. I heard the prisoner scream *Aoow* as he fell into the ditch. It only took one blow for him to collapse into the grave. By using the hoe Angkar was saving bullets - "No gain to keep nor loss to kill." Whether he was dead now or not didn't matter. Once they filled dirt into the grave he would suffocate anyway.

I had heard adults talking about witnessing executions before, but this was my first. I was nervous, trembling so much that I nearly fell out of the tree. I was afraid I would be seen, so I stayed as quiet as I could. Once they went away I carefully climbed down, still shaking. I didn't tell anyone about it. As usual, I pretended to see no evil, hear no evil and speak no evil.

Angkar had promised us independence and self-reliance, but they had also promised to look after us and treat everyone equally. There was supposed to be none of the corruption and oppression of the previous regime. They had promised peace and prosperity. Instead I was now a starving slave. We were all starving slaves for Angkar who were never allowed to rest. There was always digging to do, fields to tend and irrigation systems to build.

April 17, 1976 was the first anniversary of the Khmer Rouge victory and on this one glorious day, they told us, things were going to be different. This was an opportunity to celebrate. We were given the day off after gathering in the village to sing along to the new national anthem:

April 17th Glorious Victory!
Bright red blood
Which covers the towns and plains of Kampuchea, our motherland
Blood of workers and peasants
Blood of revolutionary men and women
The blood changes into great anger and the courage to struggle

resolutely
On the 17th of April, under the flag of revolution
The blood freed us from oppression and slavery
Victory! April 17th, the glorious victory!

The boys at the camp made a parody of this national anthem, but I can remember only the first few lines:

Bright red blood
Baby cries in mother's womb
The baby is already three months old
Mother must go and join the revolution...

For the first time since being sent to the camp we were given the day off and were free to do whatever we wanted. We could go hunting or fishing or looking for beehives or climbing trees to look for fruit. There were no bells ringing, no quotas to fill. The village was even allowed to slaughter a few old cows and pigs. We were all given a beef stew made with lemongrass and young banana trunk. We also had pork cooked in a curry with coconut milk and served with rice. After so many starving months, for once food was plentiful. The last time I had had a good meal of meat was when Grandfather Huot had slaughtered his pig.

I ate so much at lunch I could barely walk. After months of back breaking labour I was exhausted, so I went to Grandfather Huot's place for some much-needed sleep. I lay down on an old hammock made from straw with my arm over my eyes to keep out the bright sunshine flickering through the tamarind branches. I was half asleep when I felt my armpit being tickled. Probably a fly. I brushed it away. I felt it again. It was my brother Huang. I told him to stop as I was tired. He kept tickling me until I got angry and chased him all the way to the middle of the rice field. I calmed down and gave him a few playful knuckles on his head. I was happy to see him, and we talked for a while as we walked back to the house. His camp was closer to the village than mine, and because he was small and homesick, he would sometimes sneak out after dinner, running across the graveyard to spend the night with Mama. Conditions were no better for him than for me. One day he had been given his food ration on a plate with a hole. He used his fingers to try and stop the hot porridge from leaking out, but by the time he was able to sit down to eat it more than half of it was on the ground.

The anniversary day went too quickly. That night we went back to our camps, and the next day it was back to hard labour, knowing our next break wouldn't be for another year. Nobody had imagined that our time away from Phnom Penh would last this long, or be like this. We didn't realise that the glorious victory of the Khmer Rouge would be so merciless and brutal. All I could do was believe that one day the nightmare would end. Where there is life there is hope, I thought, and so I vowed to keep living, and with the vow came strength.

CHAPTER ELEVEN

THREE TONS PER HECTARE

The new Khmer Rouge's slogan I had learned in my second year was "Three Tons Per Hectare". We often chanted the phrase at our regular meeting: Three tons per hectare, Hooray! Hooray! Hooray!

And so, with the start of the new monsoon, preparation for the next year's rice crop was well underway. Before we started working a new chief of Kor Sahakor (Commune) was appointed, and the Khmer Rouge *Yothea* were replaced. The old chief was sent for *Korsang*. The new administration came with a new demand from Angkar Leu (the Upper Angkar): we had to increase our rice production to three tons per hectare so that Cambodia could become self-sufficient and self-reliance. I wasn't a skilled farmer, but three tons per hectare sounded like a lot of rice production to me. I knew enough to understand one thing, though, and that was more production would require more water - and that would mean more digging.

In most parts of Cambodia, there were two rice crops a year, although both were planted at the start of the monsoon. The first harvest took place around August and was known as the light crop, the second began at the start of the dry season in November and lasted until the end of January, and this was the heavy crop as it took nearly six months to grow - the light crop only took three or four. Angkar decided to add another harvest by planting another light crop at the end of the monsoon. I wasn't looking forward to yet more work in the fields.

Like digging the channels, we were given a quota of rice to plant: a two-metre lane the length of a rice paddy, sometimes more than ten metres long. It was back breaking work. Pulling the seedlings out was usually easy, however some of them had roots going quite deep into the clay soil. If you didn't pull them out correctly they'd break off. All the seedlings needed cleaning to some degree by swirling them in the paddy water and hitting them against your leg. If I pulled them the wrong way, however, too much mud and clay would stick to them and it would take longer to clean off. If you could work faster to reach the end of the field before everyone else finished and have a rest. That didn't happen often for me, though.

I was undernourished and physically exhausted. I was a slow worker, and frequently fell behind. I was still subject to bullying by some of the local boys and they thought it was funny to fling mud from their seedlings at me. I would soon be covered in it: on my face, my ears, all over.

Once you had uprooted enough seedlings in your row, you bundled them together and carried them to a different field for re-planting. You would always try and transplant them quickly so you could have a break, but if you didn't do it properly the seedlings would dislodge themselves and float on the water, and you would be sent back to plant them again.

The transplanting process lasted a couple of long months and was hard work. We kept at it from dawn to dusk with our feet in the mud, with only one break in the middle of the day for lunch. Whether a blazing hot day, or in a tropical downpour, it was only when we heard the bell ring that we were allowed to stop.

In the second year of Angkar, the boys in my age group became a part of the *Krom Chalat Komar* (Children's Mobile Brigade) and were sent away from Kor Village to work in distant fields far, far away from the village. We were made to build our own camps and kitchens. Our quotas became more demanding. We weren't allowed to travel, and weren't allowed to visit the communal kitchens of other villages. Our only food was what was cooked in our own kitchens. There was no more hunting or palm sap tapping. We were too far away to visit the village or see our families.

We were sent to region called Kampong Siem, about thirty kilometres from Kor Village. There, we began to clear a small hill to expand the local rice fields and build a new water reservoir. Because rice needs water, this meant we had to flatten the hill first. To make things worse, the place had obviously been the site of a mass execution as there were bones everywhere, although no fresh ones, thankfully. They were scattered everywhere in the dry hot sun, so many skeletons and skulls. It was a horrible sight, all these bones on one small hill.

We were long past the point we could pretend people had been sent for *Korsang*. The only re-education these people had received was at the end of the gun barrel or a hoe. It was even possible that these were the bones of our neighbours, of the boys and families that had been taken from Kor Village.

There were plenty of better places to grow rice, why it was necessary to flatten this hill with its mass grave was beyond comprehension. None of us dared to question the order, of course. We dug away with our hoes, casting the bones into our baskets along with the dirt. We carried them away to be buried in the bank of the dam, acknowledging that these poor souls couldn't rest in peace even after death. Perhaps the Khmer Rouge thought the hill was a good place to grow rice because the soil was well fertilized.

One day I was sent to plant rice in a paddy with water in it up to my knees. As I worked I encountered something unthinkable. I dipped my hand into the muddy water to plant my rice and hit something hard. I pushed and pushed, but my rice seedlings would not go in. I thought it must be a fresh palm fruit that was stuck in the mud, not for a moment suspecting what it really was. I dug around, trying to pull it out. It came out of the water quickly and I lost my balance and fell backwards. It was something I had now seen many times, but had never touched before. I stood up, slowly recomposing myself in this secluded corner of the field. In my left hand, I still held my rice seedlings, but in my right... it wasn't a palm fruit. It was the size of a coconut, and the muddy water dripping down from it now revealed two empty eye sockets. It was the skull of one of the poor victims of Angkar.

I had seen so many human remains in the last year that they had become part of the landscape, but this time it was different.

I was actually holding a skull. I was shivering, my breathing stopped for a few seconds. The hair on my head was standing on end and I had goose bumps. I had no choice but to quickly throw it into a nearby bush. I pretended nothing happened and just kept planting, moving away from the area as quickly as I could. My heart was racing. I was not scared of ghosts: I was frightened of death itself. I was afraid that the Khmer Rouge would kill me, for finding the skull, for not working well, for being Chinese or... for anything.

We worked diligently and forlornly through one season and into the next. The demand to grow three tonnes per hectare rang in our ears and we were constantly driven into the ground trying to make the impossible real. To get yields like that required machines, but Angkar obviously had other ideas, and believed in us more than we believed in ourselves.

If there was nothing we could use to pump water into a field, we used human powered water mills. If there were no water mills, we used buckets. These were secured to four pieces of wood, two at the top and two at the bottom. Rope was tied to the wood and two boys would stand on the bank of the river holding them. We synchronised our movements so that the bucket was lowered into the river and then swung up and into the field. Usually, because of the digging or planting or hauling water, at the end of each working day my legs and arms were very tired, and screaming with pain.

After the fields were planted we were given no chance to rest. In the old days, the farmers had a break between seasons, but in this new regime there were always other jobs to do, more channels to be dug and dams to build, all with the futile goal of three tons per hectare.

Our group was moved from one camp to another, clearing hills, chopping down forest and creating paddies where none existed previously. After travelling from place to place for a while we eventually ended up back at Kampong Siem because Angkar had a glorious new project for us: we were to expand some existing reservoirs into one large dam so we could irrigate all year round. We were ordered to work more than twelve hours per day, which was the same as the adults. We had to dig a two-by-two cubic metre hole on each shift and then carry the dirt up the hill to build up the bank of the dam. Day-in, day-out, we worked non-stop.

We would eat and as soon as it got dark we'd sleep like logs, no matter that we were inside makeshift huts with low poorly made palm leaf walls and holes in the roof. We built the huts ourselves, and we were no construction experts. The bamboo floors were only just off the ground. Our beds were low, just matting with a piece of bamboo for a pillow. Some nights, heavy rain would pour onto the fields, flooding our hut, but we were usually too tired to move and would sleep with half our bodies submerged. The chill from sleeping in the water combined with exhaustion and malnutrition, and my malaria came back. Grandma was nowhere around to offer me medicine. Instead my team leader sent me for treatment in a Khmer Rouge hospital where I was offered rabbit poo medicine. I took it - it was all there was, and I hoped it would work.

While at the hospital I met a girl. She was just a few years older than me and lived in a girls' camp far from us. Like me, she was a New Person from Phnom Penh with her hair cut short in line with her chin. Her hair was dry and messy, probably infested with lice. Every now and then she scratched her head. Her fingernails were dirty just like mine. Her cheekbones were clearly visible through skin that had become a dark olive after long hours being exposed to the sun. She lay in the bed next to me, we were two kids face to face, and we talked about everything that had happened. Although I had never worked alongside girls, I knew they were experiencing the same brutality and ruthlessness as the rest of us. She told me that Angkar's plan was for the whole of Kor Village to become mobile brigades as soon as the local work was finished. We talked more, and inevitably our conversation turned to Phnom Penh and the life we had known before Angkar. I spoke quietly about the songs and music that I used to listen to, and that I knew the song, "Beautiful Sunday". I was about to sing it to her when she reminded me, "Don't sing it here and never let anyone know that you can speak English. They will consider you *"no gain to keep nor loss to kill."*

For that very moment, I completely forgot about the ever-present danger around us because it had been so long since I had had a conversation. I was used to a world of quiet, to the relative safety of silence. That was how we lived now, with no music and no dancing and definitely no laughter. The only conversations we had these days were about quotas and pain. I could not remember the last time I had just chatted to anyone. I wore a blank look and tried to keep my heart blank as well. We were universally like that, not wanting to be noticed, not wanting to feel - and we were all just children.

Somehow the rabbit poo must have worked, because before I knew it I was back at the dam site, once more digging my quota. Then it was time to harvest the rice crop, so we were sent back to the fields again.

This was the heavy rice and it was the dry season, so harvesting the crop was easier than walking through the mud to sow it. There were some paddies in low lying areas which were still flooded. This was the "floating" rice. The water was knee high for an adult, but for kids like me was up to our waists. The water had leeches in it, and they normally fed on cattle, but for those few days of the harvest I imagined they celebrated all the human blood that was suddenly available to them. They were there in the planting season as well, but the water was only up to our ankles then and they could be easily scraped off. I think there were more of the slimy, skinny parasites at harvest time because all the other fields were dry. We'd jump in and cut the rice as quickly as we could while making as much noise as possible to scare them away. It didn't work. Leeches are attracted to motion and fresh blood, we were providing the first, and after detaching a few of them, we provided the second as well. I hated the leeches, and the Khmer boys soon picked up on this.

"Be careful, those leeches will get inside your white Chinese willy. Once they get in there you can't get them out."

I was terrified! I used straw to tie the bottoms of my trousers tightly to my legs to step the leeches getting into my pants. I worked quickly, and as soon as I was back on the bank I checked myself. I already had several leeches, some on my body and some on my thighs. One had even attached itself to one of my testicles. I pulled down my pants hurriedly to the sound of the other kids laughing. Fortunately, it was only small and hadn't been sucking very long. The one on my thigh had obviously been there longer, it was fat, about the size of my finger. It was hard to get them off - it was a bit like pulling on an elastic band - they would stretch and then contract, and they had a firm hold. The easiest way was to find some tobacco leaves, dip them in water and then squeeze the juice onto their heads. Sometimes I had no choice but to wait until they had their fill and dropped off naturally.

The harvesting season lasted for another couple of months while we cut the rice, threshed it and transported it to village warehouses. It was harder than last season. The mantra of three tons per hectare echoed in our heads as our workload increased and our rations decreased. We only had properly cooked rice for a few months before it was back to watery rice porridge again. When we had soup it hardly had any vegetables in it except for a few slices of banana trunk and a vine leaf that was normally used for pig food. The only other addition was if the kitchen staff found some mushrooms on the local haystacks, straw mushrooms[4] they were called.

I was suffering physically, but emotionally I was having trouble as well. I was really missing my family, especially Mama. At the old boys' camp, there had been the occasional opportunity to go to Grandfather Huot's house, but it had now been a year since we had moved away and my heart was aching. We were half a day's walk from the village, and without being given any time off I had had no opportunity to see her. Even

---

[4] Called chicken heart mushrooms in Khmer, because that's what they looked like. Being so hungry, we would pretend that's what they were, and they were a delicacy for us.

when I wasn't able to visit her in the old camp I knew she was nearby, and felt her presence. Without her, I was so lonely.

We were really looking forward to the second anniversary of the Khmer Rouge victory, hoping it would be a similar celebration to the first. We were told we could return to our villages, and I knew I wasn't the only boy desperate to see his family again. Some of us decided not to wait to the morning - why waste half the day walking when we could get there at night and spend more time with them?

On the eve of the second anniversary we ate our dinners even more quickly than normal, then returned to finish our quotas. It grew dark. A dim half-moon hung above us offering just enough light to see the edges of the paths that ran along the banks of the rice fields.

The local boys knew the way and we headed off, sometimes taking shortcuts across dry rice paddies we had already harvested. One of the kids with us was Pang, who lived in the hut behind Grandfather Huot's. He wasn't the group leader anymore, and he was usually kind to me. All I had to do was keep up with him. His mother was elderly and lived alone, and I knew he was concerned about her. We hurried through the night driven by compassion and homesickness. I followed closely behind Pang and we walked for a few hours in the shadows of the palm trees under the moonlight. We arrived in the village quite late and everyone was already asleep, and of course they had no way of knowing we were coming. I was so happy to see Mama, Father, my grandparents and my brothers. They were happy to see me, too. I lay down on the bamboo floor next to Mama and snuggled up to her, covering myself with my *Krama*. I soon drifted off to sleep in the breeze of a cool April night. It was the first time in two years I had slept under the same roof as Mama. I knew that tomorrow would go too quickly and that I would have to return to the camp. Right then I wanted the night to last forever.

I had the luxury of a small sleep in the next morning and finally woke to the sound of footsteps on the squeaky bamboo floor. Mama was there, sitting in silence, just watching me. She explored my young body with bitterness in her eyes. I think she had been crying. No doubt she was expecting I would have grown, but in fact the reverse had happened. With more work and less food, with even our congee rice porridge reduced to a thin gruel I was much skinnier than I should have been. I had lost a lot of weight, not that I had very much to start with. I was malnourished, with the classic sign of a distended stomach. My ribs and cheekbones pushed through my skin, and my thighs had shrunk so much my knees stuck out in contrast. The skin at the bottom of my feet was rough and thick like leather from walking without shoes for so long. My sandals made from old tyres had worn out long ago and Angkar had not distributed any more. She could also see I hadn't had a good bath in a long time. In fact, I was as dirty as a pig. I had marks on my body from the dirty clothes I was forced to wear day in, day out. I had a ring of dirt around my neck and a rash around my middle. It wasn't bad enough we were forced to endure lice and leeches, but I also had the tiny white maggots of some insect living under my waistband as well. They were itchy, but I had not sought any treatment for them, if there was indeed anything other than rabbit poo. I had not had a proper toothbrush to brush my teeth with since the Khmer Rouge captured Phnom Penh. A few of my teeth were badly decayed and some were missing entirely. If you had a toothache your only option was to tie some thread to it and ask another kid to yank it out for you.

We were kept worse than animals - at least pigs and cattle were washed at the end of the day. Mama took me down to the well. She gave me a handful of ash and said, "Brush your teeth with this, they look very dirty."

I dipped into the ash with my wet hand and then rubbed it against my teeth with my finger. Mama then washed my hair with the same ash, and finally my clothes. There was no soap at all, but at least I now had clean hair!

We went to the kitchen for lunch and I felt like a new boy. I didn't itch nearly as much as usual and the dirt on my body was gone. I felt two kilos lighter now that my clothes were properly washed and dried.

Mama and I lined up for our serving, however there was a problem. I did not have a ration allocated to me. Mama explained I had come back for the anniversary, but the staff stubbornly refused, telling her that my ration was back in the kitchen of the boys' camp, and that if I wanted any food I had to go back and eat it there. Grandfather Huot grew very upset, "He just came all this way to visit his mother for the day and you can't even spare him a bit of lunch? This is too much. You all are just too strict!" he croaked.

"Don't worry, never mind. Please just give me my ration and we'll share," Mama told them. Her ration was simply a plate of watery rice gruel not even enough for one person. This was the second anniversary of Angkar's glorious victory, however this year there was no celebration. There was no feast, no hearty stews or delicious curries.

The rest of the family came and we divided up the meagre amounts of porridge we had been given. This made Huang, very upset because I was given some of his food.

"Go and get your own ration at the camp!" he yelled at me.

Angkar had taught him not to have compassion for his family, not even his older brother. Kids like him were taught to turn on their families, even to the point of spying on them and reporting them to Angkar.

I was no better. His reaction made me angry and I punched him, and Mama had to spend time calming us both down. Hunger was driving us apart.

Lunch was soon over and I had to return to camp. It would take me a few hours to get there and if I arrived late I would miss dinner and have no food again. Soon I would return to the land of farming and digging. I can't explain what I was feeling. I was so young and I was about to be separated from my family again and return to a world of harshness, depravation, loneliness and pain. I was lucky to have lived through the second year of the Khmer Rouge regime. Would I survive the third year?

Chapter Twelve

Angkar Preparing Our Own Grave

We returned to the camp and went straight back to work the next morning. To complete the construction of the dam before the next monsoon we were ordered to dig for longer. Our lunch break was cut short and we had to work through the heat of the day. If there was enough moonlight, we would work until after midnight. One night I was so exhausted that I took the two baskets I used to carry soil with and put them down in my ditch. I lay down on them and fell asleep to the sound of digging all around me. It seemed like it was only moments later that I woke up, but by then it was dead quiet. Everyone had gone back to the huts and I was alone in the middle of nowhere. Perhaps it had just been too dark and they hadn't seen me, or possibly no one cared anymore, because we were all too tired to care. If a boy vanished no one would think about asking what happened to him. We knew the answer too well, and so the most we might say was *Min Doeng, Min Luer, Min Skal* (pretend you don't know, don't hear, and don't recognise). Once the monsoon started we were sent back to the rice fields and planted, then we were sent back to the dam to dig, when the rains finished and the crop was ready we returned to the paddies to harvest.

Since we were now a mobile brigade, we were constantly on the move from one makeshift camp to the next. Angkar deliberately sent us far away from our parents. The only time we saw anyone from the village was in 1977 at Chamkar Leu (Upper Farm), about thirty kilometres north of Kor Village, where we found some other families we knew there. It took us hours to walk through the forest and across the fields to reach our destination, and only the local Khmer boys knew the way. As soon as we arrived we started building our temporary shelter: the usual bamboo hut with palm leaf walls and straw roof. We were here to harvest a vast area of banana plantations and a few hectares of sweet potatoes and yams which had been left abandoned until now. After a hard day at work Angkar gave us rations of boiled wild yams, but sadly there were no good tasting sweet potatoes on the menu. The yams had crystal white flesh that was fine to eat, but they were flavourless. In the old days, we only ate them with sugar.

As if Angkar was not cruel enough, lack of local knowledge continued to take its toll on the New People. We only ever ate the yams after they'd been peeled, but some New People were so hungry that they roasted the skins on the fire. Although they smelled delicious they were actually poisonous, I heard that some people became ill and a few even died from eating them. Some ate wild mushrooms not knowing that they, too, were poisonous. In addition, there was a plant called Sweet Leaf which had leaves that tasted delicious in a curry, however, there was another one which looked a lot like it, so that unless you knew to look closely for the fine transparent thorns on the back of the leaf, you would think they were the same. Unfortunately, the pretend sweet leaf was also deadly. I was fortunate that the Khmer boys showed me the difference, because the highland farmers were the only ones who knew. Death was all around us, we heard of people dying all the time, death was just another part of our daily world.

After all the bananas and potatoes were harvested and transported away, the married couples and families returned to the village to prepare for the next harvest while the boys of *Krom Chalat Komar* (Children's Mobile Brigade) were sent away to do more digging.

One night I bumped into Father at the well. It was good to see him. He fetched up some buckets of water for me. Usually I was so exhausted I didn't have the strength to haul up more than a few litres, but because his buckets were full this time I was able to have a good wash, the first decent one since I had visited my parents on the second anniversary of Angkar. He told me that Mama was at the main provincial hospital looking after my brother Hun, who had diarrhoea so badly he was bleeding internally. There were a few ripe coconuts on the ground near us, put there to germinate and later be transplanted somewhere else. As soon as we had finished showering Father put a coconut into his bucket and covered it with his *Krama* and off he went, knowing that staying there with the stolen nut was too dangerous for both of us. Coconuts don't have a lot of sweetness when they are ripe like that, but to a hungry man all food is good, no matter how it tastes.

We were slowly realising that the people from Kor *Sahakor* were being forced to endure harsher and more ruthless treatment than some of the surrounding villages. Some nearby communes still had proper cooked rice, but we only had it for a few months during harvest season. In addition, the executions continued, and there had been another purge at the end of the last rainy season. One of the victims was the new chief. Angkar looked for a replacement, but this time there were no volunteers. The elders now knew that being the *Sahakor* chief was a dangerous and difficult job, which carried no real power.

It was hard to watch your friends and relatives suffering under Angkar and not be able to do anything about it. In the old days, the elders spent their evenings on each other's front porches, happily chatting. Most of them had known each other all their lives. They didn't want to be cruel to their friends. And they had seen what had happened to the first two chiefs under Angkar. While the first had disappeared, they'd witnessed the second suffer horribly at the hands of the Khmer Rouge *Yothea*. They had beaten him until he went blind, then they'd bound his hands behind his back and hitched him to a horse, before dragging him away across the rice fields, never to be seen again.

To resolve the dilemma, Angkar eventually sent us *Mett* Yong and his female companion *Mett* Meenik, a thick-faced black-hearted pair who were to oversee not just our little village but the whole province. They were in their late teens although Mama thought they were younger, and they were the first elite Khmer Rouge *Mett* I had ever seen. Up until this time Angkar's presence in the village was only through local people or the

Khmer Rouge communicating Angkar's instructions - these people were actually part of Angkar. I had sometimes tried to imagine what Angkar was really like, and I thought they were like the soldiers we had seen, with their Chinese caps, AK47s and red *Krama*.

Yong had a light olive complexion and looked like he had never worked in the sun. He was handsome, especially in comparison to the rest of us who were skinny with bony cheeks and hollow eyes. He was fit and tall and wore black pyjama style pants and a white shirt - it looked almost like a business shirt - with the sleeves rolled up, a red *Krama* around his waist and a small handgun. *Mett* Meenik wore the Khmer Rouge standard uniform of black pyjamas and the *Krama*.

It soon became apparent that *Mett* Yong was very brutal. He would order the Khmer Rouge *Yothea* to execute people after even the slightest mistake, such as accidentally stumbling into the fields and trampling some rice seedlings. Even taking a few grains of leftover rice from someone's plate was enough to have you accused of being a thief and being taken away.

We heard of New People being loaded onto trucks in broad daylight, and it was rumoured they were executed at the site of the old mass grave at Kampong Siem.

"Angkar took them right from the paddy, they were loaded onto a truck and taken away, their clothes still muddy from working," Mama told us.

Her heart was in her mouth again. If Angkar was so determined to make all New People extinct, at some stage it would inevitably be our turn.

"I was so afraid," said Mother. "I couldn't look at them. I was scared if I did Angkar would come for us, "to kill and throw away."

Mama had kept her head down and avoided eye contact with anyone, especially the Khmer Rouge *Yothea*. She said she continued to work as if nothing unusual was happening. She said that those who were rounded up walked over to the truck and calmly climbed onto it. No one put up a fight or struggled, despite the fact they knew they were being taken to their deaths.

Perhaps the fear of living had grown stronger than the fear of death. The victims outnumbered the Khmer Rouge *Yothea* but after so many years of brutality, intimidation, exhaustion and starvation, they had lost the capacity to reason. Maybe they had lost the will to fight and the will to live as well.

Once we finally finished the Kampong Siem dam, instead of returning to the village for rest, Angkar gave us the honour of more digging, this time building an extension of the existing Tuk Char reservoir, an even larger project than the one we'd just completed. *Mett* Yong turned our mobile brigades into a non-stop labour camp. Tuk Char was so large it would take years to finish. We were also given another honour: we were to be considered as adults, at least in terms of how much we were expected to do. Up to this point we'd been required to extract a daily quota of a cubic metre of soil - this was now doubled. The new quota was so demanding I don't know if I ever completed it. Our working day started very early in the morning and went late into the night, with only short breaks for lunch and dinner. We split our work, so that the Old People usually did the digging while the New People hauled the dirt up the slope. Even without a full load I found it hard to walk up the steep dam wall. Carrying two heavy baskets full of dirt with a yoke on my shoulders made me stagger from side to side and eventually I ended up permanently injuring the muscle on top of my right shoulder. It took nearly five minutes just to get to the top, while down below the diggers were having a rest until my return.

Every morning it seemed like the bell to wake us up rang earlier than the day before. We would wearily move to the assembly line. I marched to work with eyes I could hardly keep open, desperately wanting to go back to bed, but forced to follow the person in front of me. The dam was enormous, with a bank about fifteen metres high and as wide as a two-lane highway. From the top of its bank, it looked like an open cut mine. We slaved away, digging deeper and deeper and making the wall higher and higher for fourteen to sixteen hours a day, and sometimes even more. No matter how hard we worked, though, our rations remained meagre. Desperate for food, we heard rumours that Angkar was trading our rice with China for tools, guns and bicycles because we weren't producing them ourselves.

Eventually everyone from our district, including the adult brigades and a few other villagers, came to Tuk Char, except the very elderly or very young. The *Sahakor* kitchen was enlarged to accommodate everyone. It was at the end of the monsoon of 1978 when the rest of our commune as well as communes from other villages joined us until eventually there were tens of thousands of people digging day and night along the bank of a dam that stretched as far as you could see. I became aware of a new noise, the sound of thousands of hoes digging in synchronicity.

The third anniversary of the arrival of Angkar came and went with no celebration; not even a day off. It had been another twelve long months of loneliness and pain. I knew my family was here somewhere, but there were so many people I hadn't seen them in the crowd. Eventually I saw Mama, but we had few opportunities for conversation, although she was able to pass occasional messages to me.

At great risk to our entire family, Mama had managed to get some rice water. She always carried a small tin bucket which she'd use to fetch water from the well, to wash clothes in and to fetch rice water. The cooks in the communal kitchen would cook rice in large iron pans. Once the rice was boiling they would drain off some of the water and let the rice simmer. The rice water was used to mix with bran for pig food; but here in the labour camp, in the middle of nowhere, the cooks would pour it into a big bucket and leave it unattended, so that couples or families could come and take it. When *Mett* Yong heard about this, however, he put his foot down and ordered that the water be poured onto the ground. He said it showed inequality that some *Mett* could drink it while others couldn't. Knowing that people were starving, some of the cooks would turn a blind eye so that people could still take some, although others, no doubt in fear for their own lives, would refuse, saying that Angkar had said no.

Mama had a relationship with one old lady, and wouldn't take no for an answer. She politely insisted that she would be having some rice water. She placed her bucket underneath a table beside the stove and covered it with a palm leaf. "Just pour the rice water in it and I'll come and collect it later."

Mama would take her bucket to the kitchen on her way to work and would pick it up at lunch and dinner full of rice water. Whenever she saw me she'd tell me to come to her hut so I could drink some.

"I have rice water in my hut, come and drink".

I'd sneak away from my usual path to the kitchen and detour into her hut for a few sips. The rice water had no actual rice in it, but it filled my stomach for a while and helped to keep me going. I was so hungry I could easily have finished the entire bucket, but knew I had to leave enough for everyone else. My stomach was swollen, a classic symptom of malnutrition. From the side, I looked like I was nine months pregnant. All us kids were like this, just protruding bones, yellowish skin and huge distended stomachs.

Mother also told Uncle Yu about the rice water, and this ended up getting us in trouble, because he sneaked into Mama's hut once too often. Yu's team leader was a local Khmer who lived just across from my grandfather's old house. He was the older brother of Hak, the boy who had provoked me into a fight by jumping over my head while I was swimming. He noticed the regular detours and called Yu in to question him. This was serious. We were all immediately worried - after so long all our lives might finally be at stake. Fortunately, the team leader only summoned Yu and not the rest of us. We waited nervously to find out what had happened. If Yu mentioned the rice water, we were all doomed. On no account could he mention the rice water.

When Mama finally saw Yu a few days later his voice was croaky and he was in tears - and he was badly bruised. They had started by questioning him about his regular disappearances.

"*Mett*, where do *Mett* go? What do *Mett* do there? Are *Mett* being lazy and going for a rest?" his team leader wanted to know.

"I just go in for some water," Uncle Yu lied

This was the critical moment. If they heard about the rice water not only our whole family, but the woman in the kitchen and her whole family would be as dead as the bones on Kampong Siem hill. Despite a severe beating, Yu didn't say anything else. He was ordered back to work, but was given penalties by the leader. The other workers were ordered to make sure his baskets were extra heavy, full of large rocks he had to carry to the top of the bank. It should be remembered that both Yu and Hiam had been born and raised in Kor, but because they had come to Phnom Penh to live with us they were still considered to be New People. Yu in particular was treated very badly because Angkar said he had left the village to take advantage of the peasants and farmers. He was given twice as much work to do although his food ration remained the same as everyone else, despite hearing the continual mantra of "all *Mett* are equal."

I hadn't seen Yu on the work site at all, but after the beating I finally came across him. He was a lot thinner than his hippy days. His clothes were dirty and had patches everywhere. He no longer wore bell bottoms, and his shirt which he had tried to dye had faded into a murky grey, and was stained with mud. He walked barefoot with a limp, struggling to carry the weight of the heavy yoke and baskets up the steep slope. One of his ankles was bruised and swollen from a cut. He could hardly walk, let alone while carrying a load of rocks and dirt.

He had told Mama he wanted to die, but he planned to kill the leader first. He said he could face the physical pain they had inflicted on him but not the humiliation he had suffered and the damage to his pride.

"They beat me and kicked my swollen ankle. They keep putting more weight into my baskets," he said. "I don't want to live any more. I want to kill him and then take my own life."

Mother had a mantra of her own, one we had heard over

and over.

"This nightmare can't last forever. It should end someday, and until then we obey Angkar, keep our heads down and our mouths shut. We have to work hard and stay out of trouble!"

Mama wasn't ready to die yet, at least not by being taken away for execution by a hoe in a mass grave. She knew, too, that if one member of the family was called then the rest of us would be dragged along indiscriminately. She pleaded with Yu, telling him again that things couldn't continue like this forever. Someday, someone somehow would come to free us.

"Yu, listen to me, don't do it! It's not worth it. You'll risk everyone's life. You have to endure and continue with the work even if it kills you."

Her voice trembled as she begged him not to do anything stupid. In one sense, it was all right for him, he was a single man, but she had the lives of her four little boys to worry about.

"If you collapse and die of natural causes, it's one thing, but if they kill you, then it's not just your life. It's also my life, my children's and everyone else in the family, including Mae's and Pa's. Please, please don't do it. Injury or not, if you can walk you have to continue working."

She suggested he apply some natural bush herbs to his injured ankles, but he shook his head.

"No, if I let them keep getting more swollen they might get so bad they send me to the hospital and at least there I'll get some rest."

Mama was still worried. If Yu could not walk he might become one of the "since one is useless, there is neither gain to keep nor loss to eliminate" people - and that might still mean we would be dragged into a grave with him. Fortunately for us, Yu listened to Mama. Eventually his ankle became so infected his team leader had no choice but to send him to the provincial hospital for treatment.

In the three long years since the fall of Phnom Penh many people had died of starvation and disease. Other young single men and women in Yu's *Krom Chrolot*, had taken their own lives rather than suffer under Angkar any longer. Under the Khmer

Rouge there were many strict rules, and one was that "no one can have a relationship without Angkar's approval." Men and women were segregated. Kept apart in their two camps - and even if we had the time or energy - there was no opportunity to mix and mingle, there were no love affairs, dating or flirting. Couples would have been jailed, or sent for *Korsang*. Angkar made the decisions regarding relationships for us. I heard of one village where mass weddings were held twice a year, with Angkar deciding who would marry whom. In some cases, female civilians were forced to marry Angkar *Yothea*.

More and more young people were deciding they couldn't take the suffering and were choosing to end it. Maybe once one person did it, it became a realistic alternative for others, because this became a period where many young people died at their own hands. Outside the labour camp was a large tamarind tree with lots of branches. One morning I woke up to the sound of low muttering. The sky was grey and the sun hadn't risen yet. I went outside and saw a few people at the base of the tree: from the branches a boy and girl were hanging. The next morning there were more bodies there. Were they couples who felt that because there was no way they could be together suicide was the only choice? New bodies appeared in the tree for days. You could feel the presence of death lingering in the heavy monsoon air. Cambodians believe in the afterlife, so presumably these young people had faith they would be together again. Some said they hadn't committed suicide, but had been executed by Angkar and hung up there to teach us a lesson. Whether they committed suicide or were executed, though, one way or another they were dead and relieved from the constant misery and suffering.

When Angkar ordered the families to dig the reservoir at Tuk Char, Mama had moved ten kilometres from the village to the campsite. My second youngest brother, Chong - now six years old - started crying, begging her not to go.

"*Mett*, do you want him to stay here or do you want to take him with you?" the leader of his group asked my mother.

She felt that the right and safe answer was for him to stay

with his group in the village, but a few days later he ran away with another boy. They became lost, but luckily, they were spotted by a neighbour on an errand with his ox cart. He took Chong to Mama at Tuk Char, but before I had a chance to see him she requested that her team leader organise for him to be sent back to Kor Village.

"*Mett*, please take him back to Kor, he doesn't belong with me anymore. His ration is with his group, *Mett*, please take him back," Mother repeated.

There was no emotion on Mama's face when she asked Angkar to take him away, but there was a hole in her heart. She felt desperate and she despaired, but she refused to show dismay or resentment. She was well aware that a display of these emotions could cost us our lives. Under the Khmer Rouge, there was no happiness nor sadness; no yearning nor mourning and definitely no love - not even from a mother to a son. Like me and everyone else, Mama had learnt to suppress her emotions in a regime where there was no love, affection or happiness. The only thing Mama could do was hope and pray that he would be alright.

I prayed as well, perhaps we all did. We prayed that our suffering would end and that Angkar would fall, that the regime would fade away and be just another season that had ended, just another monsoon that had gone. And this was supposed to be a utopia!

Chapter Thirteen

The Thirteen Survivors

By now I had completely lost all track of time. I didn't know what day it was or even the month. Was it January or July? Monday or Friday? I lived in an endless routine. Every season was déjàvu - and daily hell was the stark reality. My essence as a person and the value of my life were reduced almost to nothing. I barely remembered what I did yesterday, and was only vaguely aware I would be doing it all again the next. The only things I knew were digging and an ever-present hunger. The only markers of change I had were that the start of the rainy season meant planting rice, and the start of the dry season meant harvesting it. In between there was just digging. There were no weekends, no rest days, and no holidays. Every day was a work day.

I stopped remembering or feeling. I was neither happy nor sad. Year 3 became Year 4 and I continued to work in the fields and at the dam. The only difference was that the workload grew harder, the conditions became harsher and there was even less food. No one ever asked, "What are we doing this for?" I woke up before dawn and worked until late at night, sometimes I would fall asleep in the ditch I was digging. It was one long continuous day that would last forever. I was numb but I wasn't numb. I felt no emotion but there was always physical pain. I knew I didn't have many reserves left. I weighted less than when I left Phnom Penh and had not grown an inch taller. My own reflection in the water mirrored the image of those refugee boys in the Chinese restaurant in Phnom Penh: filthy, dirty hair and skinny with my eyeballs caved into my skull and cheekbones stuck out from my skin. I was breathless and I wasn't going to last much longer.

We were in the middle of the fourth harvest season; we were loading harvested rice onto an ox cart - and waiting to see whether we had met Angkar's goal of three tons of rice per hectare. Tonight, like every night lately, the moon shone and the air was dry. All I could hear was the sound of people threshing, bouncing straw against wooden boards with whatever strength they had left so they could separate the rice grains from the stems. It was late and I was tired and hungry as usual. I could not wait for the shift to be over so I could go to sleep. This was the peak of the season and what we were doing at the Boys' Camp, they were also doing at Kor Village and in villages all over Cambodia, the same pattern of harvesting, threshing and storage being repeated everywhere.

Then we heard a long-forgotten sound in the distance - the noise of machine guns and grenades exploding! It was coming closer and closer. We had no idea what was happening. Our leaders sent us to our huts, awaiting instructions. The Khmer Rouge *Yothea* were in a panic and ordered us to start moving back to the dam.

"We have to escape, Vietnamese troops are coming, come on let's go to the dam," they told us. "We've already transported all your food there," they lied. "If you don't come with us, you won't have any rations."

It was sheer pandemonium. One minute they were all moving off to the dam, then next they were running towards Kor Village. It was total chaos. One thing was clear, though: we might at last be released from our eternal toil. Now that we had hope, some of the adults who were working near the boys' brigade started to resist and disobeyed orders.

The same sheer pandemonium also happened in village, because of their proximity to Highway 7, they were already free and no one was following Angkar anymore. Even those, like Mama, who had always encouraged people to put their heads down, to do as they were commanded in order to survive, no longer cared about what Angkar told them. All they knew is that Vietnamese troops were already on Highway 7 and were coming to save them.

Some people asked the Khmer Rouge about the children - about us.

"Where are the children? What happens to them?"

"Don't worry, everyone else, including the children, are already on their way to the dam. Comrades should go there as well," they were told. Some people ran off to find their families, but the Khmer Rouge ran away into the forest.

There was a tragic end to this episode, however, as not everyone who was still alive in Kor Village escaped the final killing. The distant sound of gunfire ceased for a while, and no one knew what was happening. Some people said the Khmer Rouge had come back. Many started running down the highway towards the advancing troops, knowing that this was where safety lay. Those guns which had grown quiet were the sound of liberation, the sound of freedom. It was ironic that the Khmers were running straight towards the army of the Vietnamese, the traditional enemy. But in the middle of the chaos, several Khmer Rouge crept out of the jungle and went to the jail behind grandfather's house. They opened fire, and killed everyone inside before fleeing back into the trees.

Back at the Boys' Camp I was totally confused. I was nearly at the end of my limit as it was, and barely had the strength to think about anything, even the fall of Angkar. I had no idea that Vietnam had invaded Cambodia. No one had told us we were at war. We had had no radio or communication with the outside world for the last four years. For me it was an unusual end to yet another exhausting working day. Our local team leaders couldn't, or wouldn't, tell us what the explosions were, so we stayed in the camp. While the despicable regime finally collapsed, and died around us, I was just too exhausted, and fell fast asleep.

A day after taking control of Kampong Cham, the Vietnamese troops along with a group of Khmer Rouge defectors travelled south along Highway 7 towards Phnom Penh. I learned later that the invasion was a response to continual incursions by the Khmer Rouge across the Vietnamese border. The indiscriminate killing of Vietnamese villagers and reports of wide spread human rights abuses in Cambodia had at last prompted the Vietnamese government to act. In fact, the war had been going on for a year. Some people now claimed to have heard the gunfire during the previous dry season. The Vietnamese had initially just protected their border with small incursions across our border. After a massive flood of refugees, however, they came back - with the backing of the Soviet Union - for a full-scale invasion.

They used a tactic known in Vietnamese as the blooming lotus, although in Cambodia we called it the buffalo horn. It involved sending troops in a pattern that saw them outflank and eventually surround their enemy. As a result, they entered Phnom Penh from both Highway 1 and Highway 7, and took the city within two weeks of commencing full scale hostilities so that Phnom Penh fell for the second time within four years on January 7th 1979. The success of the Vietnamese was partly due to the fact that so many Khmer Rouge surrendered. Many of them had become disloyal to the regime after hearing that friends and relatives in their home villages had been executed. Some even sided with the Vietnamese and fought against their former *Mett*.

I don't think I would have survived working in the Boys' Camp much longer. The swift victory of the Vietnamese and the Khmers who fought alongside them saved my life. I woke up that January morning to learn I had been rescued by my traditional enemy. I remembered seeing a propaganda poster back in Phnom Penh with a description: *Choh Tuk Krapeu, Laeng Leu Khla* (crocodile in the water, tiger up above), showing a Khmer farmer holding on to a rope suspended from a tree branch over a river while a crocodile with its mouth wide open waited hungrily below. The Thai were the tigers [5], the Vietnamese were the crocodiles, but it was the crocodiles who had saved us: the Khmer farmers.

It wasn't just my life, of course, it was the lives of all those who had been branded New People. The Khmer Rouge had wanted us extinct, but somehow, we had survived, although many of us, far too many of us, had died along the way and

---

5 Tiger was used as a reference to Thailand; however, people in Cambodia later began to refer to Pol Pot as the Tiger in the jungle.

been left to rot in the fields. The ultimate fall of the Khmer Rouge was reminiscent of their rise to power, because Angkar was now ousted by those same peasants and farmers who had initially welcomed it. They had been happy and relieved to see Angkar arrive, but they were even more happy and relieved to see Angkar go.

The regime collapsed like a house of cards. When the new day arrived in some sense it was a dawn for the whole country. The Khmer Rouge had fled and our team leaders called us together and told us to go home. Just like that. The Boys of the Frontier were escorted back to Kor Village by some of the adults who worked in the kitchen. I was still dazed, amazed it was all over, astounded that it had happened so quickly. We had no idea it was going to happen. The only thing I knew for certain was that I wasn't expected to go back to work that day - and possibly for a long time afterwards. Gradually our reality became more clear.

"*Youn* (the Vietnamese) came in last night."

I was starting to feel as if I had just woken from a coma. I was now fourteen but had lived with horror for four years. In my head, I was still ten years old. I was empty and had lost the ability to think because all I had known for so long was digging and planting rice and hunger and quotas and fear. For so long my priority had been survival: keeping my head down, doing as I was told and thinking of places to find food: frogs, crabs and the rats that had become so scarce.

Then I had an awful realisation. There had been so many New People boys in the Kor Village, but I couldn't see any of them now. Some had initially been with me in the *Krom Chalet Komar* but weren't with us now. I had no feeling while I understood they had all vanished while I was digging. Perhaps I was the only New People boy to have survived in the ordeal in Kor Village.

Naturally Mama was desperate for any news of me, particularly when she was told that Angkar had already moved the children to Tuk Char dam. There were rumours, which for all we know might have been true, that the Khmer Rouge were planning to execute the entire Tuk Char workforce at the dam. I was the only boy from the family who was with the *Krom Chalat Komar* (Children's Mobile Brigade). She stood outside the house watching the road, looking first one way, then the other. Huang and Chong had been in a camp close to the village, and like many of my aunts and uncles, were already home, having travelled through the madness of that night. Then Mama saw a group of boys in the distance. We had been walking for a couple of hours. She walked towards us, hopeful, eternally hopeful.

I was numb seeing her. We didn't hug - that wasn't part of our culture - instead she took my hand and led me silently home. When we arrived, I looked around at my family. I could hardly recognise them, they were all so thin and fragile. Their bodies seemed to have no soul in them. My parents had more wrinkles on their faces. My younger brothers, Huang eleven, Chong eight and Hun five, all looked exactly like me, sticks of bamboo with swollen stomachs and bony rib cages. Their knees were bigger than their thighs and all of us were filthier than the poorest Phnom Penh beggar. Their complexions were dark so I knew that they, too, had been exposed to long days outside in the sun. I realised I was in some ways looking in a mirror: what I was seeing in them they were no doubt seeing in me.

I suppose we were happy. After all this was a real joyful reunion; all thirteen members of our family somehow managed to survive three years, eight months and twenty days under the regime. Under other circumstances, there would be joys and tears but we were all exhausted after four years of hunger and hard labour, and none of us had the strength to express our emotions. Possibly we were all still stunned at how quickly everything had changed.

Chapter Fourteen

Revenge Always On Their Mind

Twenty-four hours earlier we were still under their control, now they had vanished. There were other family groups like us, bewildered and relieved, and slowly we began to accept that the Khmer Rouge had really gone. One thing that hadn't gone was our hunger. We needed food, but the first thing we did was dismantle the hated communal kitchen. Then we headed for the storehouses which were full from the recent harvest. The locks were cracked open and rice soon started flowing out the front door. Although we knew it belonged to everyone it was hard to forget four years of conditioning and there was still a sense of every person for themselves. We also knew this might be our only chance to get food for a long time. It wasn't a free for all, although it was all for free, but I won't say people behaved with their best manners, either. We took as much as we could carry.

Then, as we were loading our baskets, we heard a voice.

"Stop that! Stop taking Angkar's rice or I'll throw this grenade and kill all of you."

Mett Yong was alone on horseback, his *Yothea* nowhere to be seen. He was both brave and stupid - it was madness to think the villagers would behave the same way towards him now as they would have done twenty-four hours earlier. There was silence, and then one of the elders stepped forward.

"Yong, don't do this. Let us have the rice. Angkar's days are over."

There was another long pause. Everyone had their eyes turned to Yong. Then, surprisingly for such an arrogant ruthless thug, he turned his horse around and rode silently away. He left and the next and last time he was seen in Kor Village, it wasn't on his terms.

All the warehouses were opened and were quickly stripped of all their rice, corn, sugar and salt. People couldn't believe how much food they held while we had been starving. The villagers then rounded up the communal livestock and restored them to their original owners. Those whose owners couldn't be found were divided amongst the Old People. While this was going on, the New People made preparations to return to their homes in the city.

For a few days, there was plenty of food. If someone killed a cow or a pig, they would share it amongst the entire village. It had been a long time since we had eaten like this and it had never tasted so good. It slowly started to bring life back into my body. The way to win a boy's heart is via his stomach. Instead of feeding us Angkar had made us starve. Sometimes I wonder, if we had been looked after instead of being mistreated, whether we could have achieved three tons per hectare.

Father had spent most of his life in the city and was eager to return to Phnom Penh as soon as possible. He was concerned about Grandma Lee and the rest of his family. Had they made it to Vietnam? What had happened to his brothers and sisters? Are they alive? Had *any* of them survived? Father had faced deprivation in China when he was young, but it was nothing like what he had endured under the Khmer Rouge. After a couple of days, he packed some food and headed towards the city, desperate to begin the search for his family, but also curious to see what had happened to Phnom Penh.

Two days later he returned from his trip on a bicycle that he found to report that he hadn't been allowed to go all the way home to Kandal Market. The Vietnamese had set up roadblocks about seven kilometres from the centre of the city on all the major routes. He also told us that thousands of people were already pushing trolleys, walking towards Phnom Penh and determined to go home. He and Mama had had enough of Kor Village, there were too many bad memories there, and she agreed that we should return to the city immediately. She started stockpiling food, her precious photo albums and preparing to leave, while Father built a small wooden trailer. The local tinsmith gave him two old motorbike wheels without tyres - the same bucket and spoon maker who had seen the girl he had loved being taken away by the Khmer Rouge. He was distantly related to us and revealed how Father's grandmother had been in Kor Village as well. She had arrived a long time after us because she was so old and it had taken her so long to travel there. I remembered that back in Phnom Penh she could hardly walk on her own, I would support her by holding her hand or letting her lean on my shoulder. That was the last time I had seen her. I was not even aware she had been in the village with us all these years. She became ill and then sadly - with no one to look after her - she had died in the last year of Angkar. She had been buried without a headstone in a remote graveyard. Eventually one of her sons exhumed her remains and moved her to a cemetery closer to Kor Village. He gave her a proper funeral so she could rest in peace in a respectable manner, buried on a small hill amongst the rice fields closer to her family.

The villagers began to rebuild their lives. They started to fix their homes and repair their hearts. Grandfather Huot reclaimed his land and what was left of his old house. Everyone began bartering again, swapping goods and livestock to support themselves. (It would be another year before we saw money.) Grandfather Huot had an ox that was still capable of pulling a plough, and he swapped it with a neighbour for a couple of calves. Living through four years of the Khmer Rouge had at least taught me how to train a calf to pull a cart and get them to walk with the quick smart steps of a Spanish performing horse. I fell in love with those calves. I checked on them first thing every morning, and spent my days working with them. It was much better than having to fill a quota. I loved them so much I refused to go back to Phnom Penh with my parents. I was not ready to leave my babies behind. "I want to stay and train the calves," I protested. "They need me," I added. I would run away and hide, playing with the calves in the rice fields and making every effort to avoid the journey.

As our departure date loomed it became apparent that anger and rage simmered just below the surface of many people in the village. The horror of Angkar could not be erased overnight. So many lives had been shattered. Of two hundred New People families who had arrived in the village from Phnom Penh, only a handful had survived. Somehow our family was one of the luckiest, with all of us except for Great Grandmother Lee still alive. This did not mean we were unscarred, of course. Father called Cambodia "the land of the broken hearts." Mother would often remind us that if it hadn't been for her interventions, "they would have taken your father to kill a long time ago." Despite our recent reunion and how many of us there were, the village was still very quiet. We didn't really talk much about what had happened under the regime, although we knew we had all been through similar kinds of suffering and hunger.

Every family had its own tragedies, of course, and as people mourned and grieved, and shared their losses, inevitably a desire for reprisal reared its ugly head. The word *Sangsoek* (revenge) echoed silently in the hearts of people everywhere. Revenge was always on their mind, and so, the villagers began rounding up the former Khmer Rouge leaders. *Mett* Yong was on the most wanted list because of how brutal he had been.

One night Mama was telling us again we would be leaving for the city in the morning and I was making my plans to run away once more when we heard a commotion at the market place. Yong and Meenik had been captured. I don't know how they found them. Now they were prisoners, and some people shouted at them angrily while others sobbed at the thought of what their loved ones had undergone because of them.

The next morning when Mama and Father were busy packing I sneaked away. By now we had heard that Yong was going to be executed, and I hoped I would be able to see his head being chopped off. It was not long after dawn, the sun had not yet broken through the leaves of the mango trees. The streets were lit by silver grey morning light, and there was a large crowd armed with knives and axes ready to exact their revenge. I realised that the drama had been going on all night. I squeezed between everyone's legs and eventually managed to make it all the way to the front. There were a lot of other kids watching the villagers torturing the couple. Yong and Meenik were each tied to a pole, with a fire burning brightly between them. Their arms were bound behind them in the same fashion the Khmer Rouge used for their victims. I know it was cruel, but the villagers had no intention of killing them quickly. One by one people came forward and cut them, very slowly, little by little. Yong was receiving more punishment than Meenik. Blood dripped from their cuts and I could see from Yong's face that he was in great pain. People were chanting and shouting both in anger and excitement. It was fascinating to watch, but I should have known that Mama was already looking for me. She knew that I would be here. She spotted me sitting in the front row and called me to come away, but her voice was lost in the shouts for revenge. She finally came close enough to grab my arm and pulled me away.

"Kids aren't supposed to watch things like that," she scolded me. I had seen others die, I had seen piles of bones, and had held a skull. What was one more death? I knew better than to argue with Mama, though, and she was pulling so hard on my arm.

"Your father and your brothers have already left with the trailer. We have to hurry to catch up with them," she added. I tried once more to escape but Mama held onto to me tightly until we finally set out our journey back to Phnom Penh.

I learned later, the villagers ultimately decapitated Yong, but not before he had been slit open to reveal everything inside him, even his black heart. Perhaps it was better for me that Mother had found me before I could witness such cruelty. Meenik had been terrified and lost a lot of blood. At one point, she fainted and when she woke up she had clearly lost her mind, so she was never executed[6]. A week after *Mett* Yong was killed, they captured and killed *Mett* Churn, my Children of the Frontier leader.

The trip was like a flashback of our original exodus, only

---

6 At the time of writing she is still alive in Kor.

in reverse. Unlike last time, though, this time we had a destination we wanted to go to, with hope at the end of it. We were also travelling on the direct route so we knew it wouldn't take us as long. The main difference was that this time we were without Uncle Yu and Aunt Hiam, who were staying in the village. We slowly walked away, leaving Kor Village and its painful memories behind us.

Chapter Fifteen

Returning Home

The road was rough and rocky, long and unpaved all the way to the highway. It was even worse than it had been the last time we had come along it because it hadn't been tended to for four years. We had just arrived at one of the markets alongside the highway when the tinsmith from the village turned up and demanded his wheels back. Father and Mama spent a long time trying to convince him without any success. This meant we now had a trailer load of stuff and no wheels, and no way of carrying everything forwards. We had to set up camp while Father searched through the local garbage dumps, abandoned shops and houses for a new set of wheels. We were stuck there for five or six days at least, just ten kilometres from Kor Village, until eventually he found something that we could use - a pair of metal cogs. It took Father a little while to redesign and convert the trailer but once it was done he hooked his bike up to it and then cycled as we pushed from behind.

Our return was easier than the journey away. For one thing, this was the beginning of the dry season, so it was not too hot or wet. There were also far fewer people on the highway. And there were no hostile checkpoints and no Khmer Rouge moving us along. We had our hearts set on getting home as soon as possible, so it didn't take us nearly as long to reach the ferry port at Prey Kdam on the Tonle Sap River, about thirty kilometres Northwest of Phnom Penh.

This was one place where the road was congested because there were so many other families already waiting there. We had to camp for a couple of days and keep our place in the queue. Once across the river we continued south on National Highway 5 towards the city. More and more people were crowding the highway, all heading to "home sweet home" after so long away. The crowds grew thicker and thicker, and the line moved more slowly, until eventually it stopped altogether.

Many still hoped to reach home as early as possible and reunite with missing relatives as the scale of the genocide was not yet fully apparent. Unfortunately, the situation with the Vietnamese hadn't changed since Father's previous visit, and they maintained their checkpoints and barricades on all major roads and highways stopping people from entering the city. The closest point that we could get to was about six kilometres from the city centre: Kilo Six. Only the new Cambodian government officials and the Vietnamese troops were allowed inside. No reason for the impasse was given, other than there were no essential services like water and electricity, which meant nothing to us because they weren't available on our side of the barricades, either. Although the basic infrastructure had failed, many parts of the city were like a museum and hadn't been touched by the Khmer Rouge. Cars, clothes, money, gold - everything - had been ignored by them. The real reason the Vietnamese were keeping us out was so they could collect all the valuables and transport them to Vietnam. Some said it was because there was a huge stockpile of Chinese weapons and ammunition at the airport that had to be moved before we could come back.

Thousands and thousands of people now lined the highway from the Kilo Six roadblock right back to Kilo Thirteen and beyond, all living under the trees and abandoned houses, and fetching water from the river for cooking and drinking. Our family settled down to camp around Kilo Ten, setting up a temporary shelter while we waited. We all camped like the refugees we still were, sleeping on straw mattresses and sheltering under mosquito nets. Once again, we cooked on the side of the road with whatever food we had. During the day, there was not much to do, so my brothers and I would play in the Tonle Sap River. I washed my clothes and went to the toilet in the water, too, then walked a few metres upstream to get a bucket of drinking water. I naively assumed the water upstream would be clean, although looking back I'm sure everyone else assumed the same.

We waited on the fringes of the city for a few months until

inevitably people began to run low on food and firewood. While some had come with whole carts full of rice, others had arrived with not much at all. People searched for food in nearby abandoned factories and warehouses. Others had been sneaking into the city at night. There was a swamp – at this time of year it was almost dry - which you could travel through to avoid the Vietnamese checkpoints, although you had to negotiate long grass, thick scrub and barbed wire. Once inside, however, some people hit the jackpot: finding houses and stores with stockpiles of canned food, clothes and other valuables sitting there neglected. As news of the treasures filtered through, everyone wanted to try their luck. While shops and houses had remained untouched by the Khmer Rouge, this was about to change. Some people went back to their old homes and retrieved gold and other valuables they'd stashed away before the evacuation, but many others raided and looted wherever they could. Eventually the Vietnamese found out what was going on and sent out more patrols at night, warning us that they would shoot on sight. Sometimes they apprehended people and confiscated their goods, others were not so lucky and were shot and flung into the Mekong River.

Despite the danger, people continued to risk their lives, although soon the nearby houses had all been emptied and people had to travel further each night. Desperation and greed motivated men, women and children, but the rewards could be great. If you were lucky you could end up very rich. As one route into the city closed another would open. At one point, it was via the river. People would get as close as possible to the watchtower, then enter the water and swim across below the old broken bridge. Others took the reverse route, entering by land and leaving by the water. My younger brothers and I took our chance and went to the city on more than one occasion in search of our fortune. Unfortunately, all the places we visited had been looted before we got there. The best we could manage was a few sticks of firewood. My brother, Chong, was a better swimmer, he would swim across beneath the bridge with a bundle of firewood while I could hardly keep myself afloat. One night we met a man who found a warehouse full of textiles. He wrapped as much as he could around himself, and carried two more bolts of cloth over his shoulder. I was jealous and thought to myself: *why can't I find something valuable like that as well.* Tragically, he didn't make it back. Although it was only a short swim the current was strong and the weight of the water in the cloth dragged him under. On another night, I was inside a darkened house when I came across a hole in the floor. I thought my luck had changed! Maybe it was full of gold. I put my hand in and felt something that was dry on the outside but with a soft interior. Quickly I took my hand out again - I had realised what it was. It was something I remembered well from fertilising the vegetable garden: sticky, smelly human shit. Perhaps someone had left it as a present for future raiders like me. I should have known better than to think I could find gold hidden in someone else's house.

With the sudden availability of precious metals, goldsmiths popped up everywhere. We all became gold experts, able to tell good quality from inferior. Even I could do it. You would bite it to see how soft it was, or drop it on the ground and listen to the sound it made. Pure gold doesn't bounce well off a hard surface because of its relative softness. Necklaces and rings were melted down into small usable leaves that we could trade with. Small markets began to spring up along the side of the road, with rice and gold the main currencies. People who did not have gold, like my family, used their rice to barter for fish and vegetables with the boat people by the river bank. As more goods were smuggled out of the city, villagers and fishermen from across the river started arriving every morning to sell fresh produce. A large central market was soon thriving. Capitalism had been reborn.

Mama and Father didn't have any gold, but it wasn't for want of trying. Father had been to the city, and he wanted to enter the city again. He wanted to take his bike with him. Mother was against the idea, Father argued he could travel further and faster with it. Mama gave up arguing in the end, but insisted he take Huang with him. Father rode up to the checkpoint most days to find out if there was any news regarding our return to the city, and had developed a relationship with the Vietnamese soldiers there. Somehow, he got past the checkpoint and went all the way to the central railway station, but then he came across a group of Vietnamese troops having a party in the afternoon. He greeted them, a costly mistake; he had nearly been killed on this trip. These troops were drinking and possibly spurred on by the women they were with, they were not as friendly as those at Kilo Six. They captured Father and Huang, and locked Huang inside an empty train wagon while they interrogated Father and beat him up. Despite his fluent Vietnamese he could not rescue himself; the Vietnamese wouldn't let him go.

"I could hear Ah-Pa's voice and the soldiers were shouting at him in Vietnamese for a long time, then suddenly the shouting stopped. I thought they had killed him," Huang told me later. "I was scared and it was very hot inside the train wagon, so I started crying and crying, and called out Ah-Pa! Ah-Pa!"

Eventually one of the soldiers must have been sober enough to realise a child was suffering. He let Huang out from the steaming, sauna-like wagon and Father was free to go - but the damage was already done. There was blood on Father's face and bleeding came from his mouth. He was shaken and speechless; not a word was uttered as he kneeling down to pick up his broken teeth from the dirt. The Vietnamese must have hit him very hard with a hard object or the back of the AK-47 barrel. His teeth were still intact after four years under the Khmer Rouge regime without any dental care only to get them knocked out by a few drunken Vietnamese soldiers. They also confiscated the bike. Mama was furious when they came home, not just because they were nearly killed by drunken soldiers but because the bike could have been traded for an ounce of gold. That would have been enough for Mama to buy goods to start trading with again. We'd already been offered the gold for the bike, although Father had refused saying, 'Having that bike is like having a car.' We had only brought 30 kilos of rice with us, and that had to feed six mouths - and Mama had become pregnant, so soon there would be seven.

Since we had been on the road, our diet mainly consisted of sliced cucumber and eggplant dipped in a bowl of out-of-date *Prahok* (Cambodian anchovies) served with rice. *Prahok* is a small river fish salted and fermented for several months. It smells rotten but tastes delicious, and is often used in traditional Cambodian cuisine. Father had found it in an abandoned house and despite its age we relied on it, combined with our rice, in order to survive. We weren't eating much better than we had under the Khmer Rouge, although we weren't being forced to work in a labour camp, of course.

Our rice supply was starting to run low. Mama used some of it to trade with, and with her usual skill sometimes managed to make enough profit on a deal so we could buy fresh fish to cook into a soup with tamarind leaves. To help things Father set up a bicycle repair shop while I stopped sneaking into the city and began buying fruit and vegetables from the boats coming across the river in the morning, selling them in the market to help the family's finances.

By July 1979, Mama was more than six months pregnant. One morning, a man drove up to us in an ox cart. He squinted his eyes through a pair of badly broken glasses which were tied together with string. We hardly recognised him. He was with an old lady. It was Small Uncle and Grandma Lee! The night we had found the *Prahok* we had run into one of our old Kandal Market neighbours. He and Father had spoken briefly, but not being the place for a long catch up, they hadn't talked for long. The man had owned a restaurant opposite Mama's market stall, so he knew us quite well. When he had subsequently run into Grandma, he had told her that he met her son and we were near the Kilo Ten mark. We hadn't seen her or Small Uncle since they had split up from us on the exodus from Phnom Penh at the Korki market.

Grandma Lee and the rest of her family had never reached Vietnam. They had spent a month on the road but had only made it as far as Neak Leoung, about seventy kilometres from

Phnom Penh where the Khmer Rouge had forced them into a small village on the east side of the Mekong River. There was no food for New People, so they had to live on whatever they could find in the paddy fields and bamboo shoots. The village was flooded and disease ridden like in Kor Village. Sadly, Small Uncle and his wife, Keang, lost all three children. One died on the road in June 1975, the other two died six months later from malaria and diarrhoea. Although they had another son, Chou, late in the regime, Keang suffered greatly from depression and had nearly gone insane. She could no longer speak properly, although she had learned to curse fluently in Khmer.

My Grandpa Lee, that elegant old Chinese man, more a scholar than a labourer, died in January 1976, and Aunt Muy's husband had passed away not long after that as well. The rest had survived, though, including Muy's four children and my other two aunts, Hun and Heng. Only Second Uncle and his family were unaccounted for.

In some ways, Grandma Lee had been fortunate. After spending approximately a month in the village at Neak Leoung, the family had been sent to the northeast of Cambodia, because of the bombing along the Ho Chi Minh trail, there was a much smaller Khmer Rouge presence in this area. Some of the village leaders were even the New People, and families were still able to barter food and sometimes cook at home. My aunts would pretend to be ill to avoid working in the fields, and none of them were sent to join the mobile brigades as we had been. In contrast to Kor Village, many of the New People in this area had survived, including Uncle Yu's gold dealer widow.

When Mama took Grandma inside our little shelter on the side of the road to see Father again she was amazed that he was still alive. She had dreamed, he had come to call on his father just before Grandpa Lee had died, and thought this meant Father was dead, too. She was very glad to be proved wrong.

After the reunion, we went with Grandma to stay with the rest of the family under an old stilt house near Kilo Six, along with many other people sheltering from the monsoon. We had no beds, and instead simply put our straw mattresses on the ground, and covered ourselves with a mosquito net. Inevitably, however, the old frictions between the Lees and Mama appeared again, not helped by having so many people living together in such a small confined space. Although absence had initially made the heart grow fonder, soon tensions began to rise, and once again we heard how Mama had never been fully accepted because she was just a Khmer girl from the village and they were the classy Chinese from Phnom Penh.

We had been apart for four years living in our separate forms of hell and Mama was still being treated as an outsider. Even though she was pregnant they couldn't help themselves and taunted her, particularly Muy and Heng. Mama found it hard to fetch water from the river. Although it was only a few metres from where we were staying, the river had a steep slope which was difficult for her to climb up. Heng became frustrated with Mama's efforts and started being very rude, calling her a "big fat belly lazy woman". Father was helpless, Mama was his wife but they were his sisters. We hoped we wouldn't have to stay together too long and that the new government would soon let us back to our homes.

Chapter Sixteen

$$7 - 3 = 4$$

In the early months of 1979, only skilled workers like engineers and electricians were allowed to settle in Phnom Penh so they could reconstruct the city's water and electrical systems with the help of the Vietnamese engineers. Workers also started to resurrect factories that had been idle for the past four years. They were paid in Vietnamese rice, and only these employees and Vietnamese troops were offered housing, the rest of us still had to make do with huts or shelters beneath houses like we were living in at Kilo Six. It wasn't until almost six months later that the barricaders were removed and we were allowed back into the city.

So much looting had occurred that by the time we were finally let back inside the city everything was gone. It had all been stripped and skinned to the bone. Even the old cinema where I had squeezed between adult legs to buy tickets for Bruce Lee's movies was now devoid of seats. The only thing left was graffiti, and, oddly enough, the maths equation "7 - 3 = 4" scratched in charcoal on the wall. As I stood there in the pile of rubble it dawned on me that Cambodia used to have a population of seven million. Three million had died - the same as the entire population of Phnom Penh before the war. So many of these were the "no gain to keep, no loss to kill" New People. I was jolted, but felt lucky to be alive. Whether this was the true figure I didn't know for sure, but from all the horror I had witnessed I could only believe it was correct.

I finally made it as far as our old house in Kandal Market. Here, too, there was nothing left - and of course there was no sign of Lily's three little abandoned puppies. I suddenly become very sad thinking of Lily. I had to bite my lip and hold back my tears as I continued looking around. The Pepsi Cola factory was in poor shape, and our old place was just a pile of broken bricks and concrete, with a few banana trees growing in the rubble. The block of apartments in front of us was intact, but was empty.

It was all too quiet. I wanted to feel the energy that used to light up the city at night just a few years before. Phnom Penh had been a place overflowing with life, full of markets and tinkling bell from passing ice cream rickshaws, the yodel of Khmer women selling noodles, the shouting of hawkers, the raised voices of Chinese merchants making deals, even the garbage man's howl: "Anyone have an empty bottle to sell? *Eleee*!"

I wanted these sweet sounds again, I wanted life to return. I wanted to hear the noises of people setting up the market in the morning, the cyclo-rickshaw riders dropping off their deliveries with a raucous cling-cling of their bicycle bells. I longed to see the stall holders lighting their cooking fires. In one corner of the market fisherman's wives used to line up with buckets of live fish caught only hours earlier. They'd loudly compete against each other to sell the fish before they died, because once dead they'd have to discount the price heavily. Villagers would bring in fresh fruit and vegetables every morning. Butchers would prepare pork and beef overnight, while chickens and ducks would be still alive. Every now and again a rooster would crow loudly and echo across the market: Coo Coo Cooooo.

As well as the sounds and sights of the markets there were the smells of spices and cooking. As you'd walk along you'd pass food stalls selling all kinds of things and they'd make your stomach rumble. There'd be Chinese fried noodles, Khmer curries and Vietnamese pancakes and spring rolls, roasted crickets with honey and frog's legs with lemon grass. The Chinese rice porridge with pig's blood and intestines that I used to have for breakfast with Grandfather sounds bad, but I can tell you that it tasted a whole lot better than the gruel we ate under the Khmer Rouge. My favourite market dish was noodle soup served with pork mince and beef meatballs, a pinch of spring onions and bean sprouts. The Chinese called this unique dish Phnom Penh Noodle. On a warm afternoon, after a dish of soup, I would tear a riel note in half to pay for an ice cream or some shaved ice with condensed milk topping to keep me cool. Homemade sweets were everywhere. I could walk where I wanted in the city, or sometimes I would ride in a cyclo-rickshaw to buy lollies and games from the New Central Market. I played in the gardens of the palace and if I'd saved enough money I'd go and see a Chinese Kung Fu movie at the cinema.

It was a child's dream playground. There were festivals all year around. Because of my Chinese and Khmer heritage, there were two events that I looked forward to every year. The first was the Chinese New Year festival which kick started the annual calendar every February, celebrated at the Chinese Buddhist temple. There would be lion dances and parades through the streets. The dancers would go from shop to shop to chase away evil spirits and bad luck for the rest of the year. In exchange, they would take red envelopes stuffed with cash hidden inside lettuces tied up with red string hung above the ground. We, kids, also received these red envelopes from our relatives and friends as a new year's gift.

In April, we celebrated the Khmer New Year where we'd pray and have traditional games and dances at the Wat Phnom temple. There were many other festivals as well before the year wrapped up with the Cambodian Water Festival known as *Bon Om Touk*. This would feature boat competitions, and we'd line the banks of the Tonle Sap River to watch the rowers race upstream towards the lake.

Phnom Penh had been the most beautiful city, our capital and a jewel of Asia, but now it was reduced to nothing. Not even ghosts walked around the dead city. It was a city of ruins. Grass and weeds had conquered, the shops were empty and the houses had no soul. No one had tended Phnom Penh for four years. Amongst the decay and dilapidation, the only new things visible were Vietnamese barbed wire barricades.

I went to pay a visit at the Tuol Sleng prison when it opened to the public. This had been a high school in the old days. The prisoners were no longer there, however, the odour of death lingered, and the bloodstains on the tile floor seemed very fresh. Many of the prisoners had been Cambodian "elites": scholars and professionals who had been tricked into returning from overseas in 1975, lured back by pleas from the Khmer Rouge.

"Angkar needs your help to rebuild Cambodia after the American bombings." As soon as they arrived they were loaded onto military trucks and sent to the prison. I sighed with thoughts of what these poor people had endured. I had heard the cries of victims being tortured in the jail behind my grandfather's house, but I had never seen what sort of conditions they had lived in. When the Vietnamese had arrived, they had taken extensive photographs of what they found there. On the cell walls was a pictorial account of extensive torture and interrogation. I saw how one poor soul had suffered, chained onto an iron bed with no mattress. Of all the corpses and skeletons that I had seen since April 1975, these were the worst.

It had only been four years, but it felt like longer. Over two thousand years of Cambodian culture, tradition and our way of life had been destroyed. It would take ten years or more to restore the city to its former glory.

I continued to trade groceries at Kilo Six market, but there was a lot of competition, as anyone with rice could barter for vegetables and fish. And there was already corruption, where police officers, who would call themselves tax collectors, would turn up out of nowhere and demand a percentage of your takings. If you refused they would confiscate your goods. It wasn't so bad if you had a proper stall and had spare rice to pay them with, but I was just a small-scale seller with one basket of things for sale. If I was lucky my entire profit for the day might be a kilo of rice, although often it was much less. The other small sellers were in similar circumstances. Any confiscation could mean the loss of our entire day's profits. Every time we saw the officers coming we'd grab our baskets and run, like rats leaving a sinking ship.

As the competition from other sellers grew, I thought I'd

try my luck closer into the city. It was about a five kilometre walk every day to reach the houses of the official residents, but once there I found the same problem with "tax collectors." It was a game of cat and mouse, of running and confiscation. If I saw them coming I could sometimes get away, but if I was in the middle of a transaction I had no chance. However, while I was selling in Phnom Penh, though, I spotted a new opportunity. I saw some men carrying boxes of ice from the city to sell at the markets, and I decided to try my hand at it. I asked father to build me a bicycle that was my size with a rack on the back that would fit a wooden box full of ice. As soon as I was mobile I headed into the city to stock up. I became the youngest ice trader.

I also had another business on the side around this time. The Vietnamese military trucks moving in and out of the city often stopped at the roadside looking to buy goods. The hawkers tried to sell them everything: fish, vegetables, coconut juice, but what they were really interested in was chicken. The Vietnamese loved chicken, and they knew we were desperate for food. They came loaded with good quality jasmine rice, still in nylon bags with a blue and green stripe. I realised this was a great business opportunity and I began trading live chickens with them. I quickly learnt Vietnamese phrases and how to count in Vietnamese. I also learned that the Vietnamese troops preferred young chickens below laying age - they were more tender. They would always look under the tail feathers to see whether the chicken had started to lay. If they thought the chicken were too old they wouldn't buy them. I learned how to do this as well, so that every morning after finishing my ice run I would buy as many chickens as I could from the villagers, paying them with good rice. The troops did not bargain like we had to, I guess they had rice to spare, so it was nothing for them to take my entire stock and drop a 50-kilo bag of rice at my feet in exchange.

Those bags of high grade rice helped prop up the ice business, which had gotten off to a rocky start. Despite waking up at 4am, I would frequently be too late and would find that most of the ice had already been sold. Many of the traders already had their regular customers and all that would be left for me were a few small leftover pieces. The time it took me to gather enough stock had a flow on effect, because it meant that when I arrived at the market I would find all my competitors had beaten me back so that most of the ice stands already had enough stock for the day. Sometimes I was forced to wait in the hot sun and sell to the general public. Naturally, as the day went on my ice started to melt. Sometimes I would lose half my stock like this, at other times I would be forced to return home and sell door to door to try and cover my costs.

One very hot day, I had a lucky break when some shaved sellers ran out of stock and came to me to replenish their supplies. Perhaps they took pity on a lonely boy standing there in the sun. After a few days, I established a relationship with them, and promised them that if they bought from me I would undercut their competitors.

I also promised that I could supply enough ice to last them through the whole day. Now that I had regular customers I needed to find a reliable supplier. Because of my high-quality rice (most of the rice at this time was broken and discoloured) I had something to trade with. I found a supplier, a doctor in the city who promised me her entire ice stock. She was not a professional ice manufacturer, it was just that the new residents had electricity and refrigerators that could make ice which they could use to trade for food. Because they were the first in the city some had two or three fridges which they used to make ice in plastic containers and tin bowls of all shapes and sizes.

In time, I found other ice makers as well, and I asked them all to supply their ice only to me. In exchange, they got good quality rice. I took all their ice no matter if the weather was hot or cold. I knew my customers would not necessarily sell all the ice I had to offer on a rainy day, but knew as well that it was important for me to be reliable. If I lost a little bit sometimes that was the price I had to pay - it meant they kept buying from me. I would wake up very early when the roads were still dark and head into the city. Mama had made two bags which I took with me, one for good rice and the other for Cambodian quality. I had to do two trips every day because I couldn't carry my entire stock in one load. It was good for a while: trading rice for ice.

Mama started trading my profits for gold, and began to expand her own business, selling everything from petrol to liquid soap. The soap was so strong that one day when I washed my hair and some got in my eyes I thought I had gone blind. I couldn't open them. Grandma Lee had to take me to a doctor and have them washed out with some special liquid.

A few months later, Small Uncle was offered a job at a garment factory at Kilo Four and was given a two-storey concrete place with electricity nearby. Father built a tin hut for us there and we moved his bike shop over the road from the house. Once the new baby was born, we were finally able to move away from Grandma's family. The hut only had one room, but at least it was home.

Not long after we moved I met someone who claimed to be the brother of Khieu Samphan, Khmer Rouge Brother Number Four. He was tall and blind in one eye. He claimed he had lost the eye due to the Khmer Rouge. He said he had never liked his brother's ideology. He had suffered greatly under Angkar, despite his family profile. It just showed how everyone's life had been affected, young or old, New People or Old People. It had scarred everyone.

I think it scarred Small Uncle - although he already had a temper. One afternoon we had a minor argument over the electricity and whether the wires coming to our hut from his house were safely connected. He grew very angry with me and hit me on the head with a bamboo pole. Father saw it happen, but couldn't intervene because of the risk Small Uncle would cut off our power, or maybe kick us out altogether. It wasn't the only time he was to be this violent with to me.

My ice selling business was going well, but the competition was building. Now that he had electricity, Small Uncle wanted to get in on it, and planned to build an ice maker from an old refrigerator he'd found. I always knew it could not last forever, and one day disaster struck. I was late and in a hurry, and hadn't strapped my ice to the rack properly. As I rode my load moved, the strap broke, the ice fell and I fell with it - and the metal on the edge of the ice box cut me deeply behind my left knee. I was bleeding when I went back to the doctor who was my ice supplier. She bandaged it up, but I had to hire a cyclo-rickshaw to take me, my bike and the ice home. It took me several weeks to recover and in that period, I lost my customers.

    I tried to revive the business but a new ice factory had opened and was providing better quality ice than domestic refrigerators could. The Vietnamese military trucks were still moving in and out of the city, but they were stopping less frequently as there were now markets established near their base camps at Battambang. The market at Kilo Six had now become the largest market in the area, and since we had moved to Kilo Four it made it difficult to trade from there. Luckily, Father was offered a job as a truck driver for the new government, so Huang, Chong and I took over his bicycle repair shop. Three boys running a shop in competition with others along the road provoked comments like, "do these kids know what they're doing?"

    "Of course, you don't have to worry. They're very good at it," Mama replied.

    Fixing bikes and mending flat tyres with my younger brothers was fun, but it didn't pay very well. Our usual customers were country travellers in need of air for their tyres or grease for their chains after a long ride on a dusty highway. They usually had little to offer as payment, perhaps only a handful of rice. The bicycle repair business was so bad and with more repair shops opened, Huang and Chong often deliberately threw nails onto the highway hoping that we'd get a few more customers to keep us busy. I had learned a lot about business by now, though, so whenever Grandma had me escort her across the border to Ho Chi Minh city to see her relatives in Vietnam, I took the opportunity to buy up on Vietnamese tyres and accessories and sell them at the repair shop.

    A year had gone by since we had returned to Phnom Penh.

We were so close, but still had not reached our old home at Kandal Market. Mama and Father had seen what state it was in, and gradually concluded that Kilo Four was where we would stay. I spent most of my time on the side of the road trying to make a living with the bike shop while Mama struggled to make small profits from selling things at her market stall - a lot of which had been smuggled out of the formerly deserted city.

Since I now had a bike, every now and again I rode to visit my grandparents in Kor Village. More of the old ways of life gradually were returning to the village, but painful memories still lingered. Parents of children, some of whom were already past the prime age of marriage - between sixteen and twenty - began to arrange for them to have weddings, including Yu in April 1979 and Hiam a few months later.

Meanwhile Grandma Lee was slowly coming to the realisation that her missing son, my Uncle Yuen, was dead. We had heard nothing of him after all this time, but of course we had no way of knowing his ultimate fate, or the fate of his wife, their five daughters and one son. They must have died either by execution or illness, as part of that awful equation: 7 minus 3 equals 4.

Phnom Penh, 1979: Our tin-house at Kilo 4, outskirts of the city.

*Uncle Yuen's children, my cousins, five girls and one boy:
Two in front row and two at the back from the left, one girl and a boy in front on the right.*

Chapter Seventeen

Father's Last Advice

A year and a half after the Pol Pot regime was ousted by Vietnamese invasion there were still some areas in the west and northwest of Cambodia where the Khmer Rouge maintained pockets of resistance and carried out acts of guerrilla warfare. The Khmer Rouge was still seen as the legitimate government of Cambodia by the UN and there were rumours they were still being supported by the US and the Britain who saw them as a useful ally against the Vietnamese communists who had invaded Cambodia. It was amazing to us that after all they had done they had any legitimacy with anyone, let alone the UN. It was as if Hitler had been pardoned! They had retreated to a region near the Thai border, herding some villagers along with them to act as human shields. Afraid of being caught in the crossfire between the Khmer Rouge and the Vietnamese, other villagers from the northwest fled their homes to take refuge in camps along the Cambodian-Thai borders. Two of the better-known camps were Camp 007 and New Camp; both were set up under the protection of the newly installed Vietnamese backed Cambodian government. The Khmer Rouge also had their camps in this region which were tolerated by the Thai government as well, figuring they would act as a barrier between Thailand and a possible continuation of Vietnamese expansion. After all we had endured under the Khmer Rouge, many of us were terrified they would one day return and continue the unfinished work they had started. The suffering people had endured under the regime had left an indelible scar in so many hearts, including mine. A trickle of refugees crossing the Thai border rapidly turned into a flood.

In Phnom Penh, the instability and insecurity was causing concern among many Cambodians, particularly the ethnic Chinese minority. It was now we started hearing about Heng Samrin, who had led the Vietnamese troops into Cambodia.

Although he had saved us from the Khmer Rouge, rumours were surfacing that he wanted to send the Chinese back to the camps so we could continue the work of Angkar. This was apparently because of a belief that Angkar was being supported by Chinese arms and money. The Vietnamese were more allied with Russia, and were no fans of the Chinese, especially after an incursion by the Chinese across the North Vietnamese border not long after the Vietnamese invasion of Cambodia in February 1979, ostensibly to put pressure on Hanoi to leave Cambodia.

When news of the refugee situation and the famine in Cambodia reached the world, international aid organisations such as the Red Cross and UNICEF sent rice to help the refugees along the Cambodian border. The 50-kilo bag of rice that the Vietnamese troops gave to me in exchange for chickens might have come from this contribution. The Khmer Rouge was also given food by the agencies meanwhile many of us in Phnom Penh were still starving.

Because so many people were fleeing the country, a formal refugee camp was established in the Prachinburi province of Thailand, known as Khao-I-Dang (or KID). It processed applications for resettlement in countries like America, France, Canada or Australia where people would have a chance of rebuilding their shattered lives. As the guerrilla warfare continued desperate people kept escaping into Thailand hoping for a ticket to freedom. We had just been rescued from hell but our memories of it were fresh, and the thought of being returned to the conditions we had known under Angkar was terrifying. Those who had relatives overseas and still had money tried to escape to Thailand.

I wanted to leave, too, but I had nowhere to go to. I knew no one overseas and more importantly, I had no money. While I was escorting Grandma Lee to Ho Chi Minh City, however, I learned that Grandma Lee and my aunts started planning their escape.

Grandma had reunited with one of her nephews. He and his family were heading to Ho Chi Minh City because his brother, who had left Cambodia before the Khmer Rouge arrived, was now living in America. He was hoping the brother would sponsor his family's visas to the US. Grandma arranged for my Aunt Hun to go along with him, hoping that she could escape to America.

Grandma was a very protective mother, and being concerned about Aunt Hun she would sometimes send Father to check on her where she was staying with her relatives. Sometimes when Father was busy with his work, she would go there herself, and I would occasionally accompany her. Several months passed without Aunt Hun securing a sponsor. Grandma's nephew in the States was refusing to help her because he was working on getting his own immediate family out. Grandma decided that the best thing was for Aunt Hun to return home. It was easy to cross the border into Vietnam at this time, with no requirement for a passport or other travel documents.

At this point, it was the same with Thailand, and traders could get in and out reasonably easily. You could travel up there by train or by getting a lift on an army truck. Some refugees in Thailand would even return briefly to Cambodia to trade, and would report news of lucky families who had been resettled overseas. The news of possible escapes via Thailand and then onto America or France brought new hope to many of us, especially when word filtered through that many had been granted visas without sponsorship. People who could not get out via Vietnam now turned their eyes to Thailand and more and more of our friends and neighbours would bid us farewell and be gone the next day, heading to the border.

Grandma's nephew and his family ultimately returned to Phnom Penh as well, after realising their only chance of escape in that direction was to become one of the "boat people" and sail across the Gulf of Thailand or the South China Sea. Thousands had made it out this way, thousands of others had drowned trying. He came to tell us he was going to head for the refugee camp in Thailand.

As with anywhere, but especially in Cambodia in those days,

if there was a need then inevitably someone would find way to profit from it. Soon unofficial travel guides began to assist people to leave. They were known as *Nyak Noum Pluo* (people who lead the way.) Today we would call them people smugglers. With so many people wanting to leave Cambodia their business was soon booming.

People smugglers worked in groups of five or six. One or two were based in Phnom Penh to collect money and let people know when the next trip out would be. They kept their eyes and ears open, especially amongst the ethnic Chinese. Another was based in the refugee camp, and would provide insight on conditions there and assist the refugees once they arrived. The rest of the team accompanied refugees on the journey from Phnom Penh to Thailand. Of course, there was a price to pay, with gold changing hands for each person they escorted.

After Hun returned to Phnom Penh, a man named Eng-Meng came to offer assistance. He was a friend from the old days. Grandma knew his parents back in Phnom Penh and they had endured the Khmer Rouge together while staying in the same village. Eng-Meng had a place in the refugee camp in Thailand and he convinced Grandma that he should take Aunt Hun and Heng back with him. Eng-Meng wasn't part of a team and preferred to work alone. He said he only came out to help friends and relatives while he was waiting to be resettled himself. Grandma wondered how much he would charge to take Aunt Hun and Heng back with him. Mama said, "It isn't money he's after, it's Heng!" This wasn't the time to be talking of marriage, however, and so a price was set.

Grandma was not just very protective but was also a very cautious mother, so even though they were in their twenties, before she handed over her daughters to Eng-Meng she told him she wanted to travel north herself to see whether it was safe and how easy it was to cross the border. I had been up there to Battambang buying tyres before. This was a one day trip, I left in the morning and returned by the evening.

There were only two kinds of people travelling north at that time: those who were going to Thailand to trade, and those who were fleeing Cambodia to seek freedom. The train carried rice convoy to and from the international aid organisations; sometimes it got hijacked by the Khmer Rouge. Despite the danger, the trains were packed, and the only place I could find for the journey was the roof of the wagon. I must say that the view from the top of the train was beautiful. At each stop, hawkers would rush to the side of the track to sell us palm fruits, coconut juice, rice wrapped in lotus leaves and local delicacies like grilled frog legs and roasted crickets.

The people who were leaving stood out clearly. While traders travelled alone with only the shirt on their back and a *Krama*, the refugees carried their most precious belongings and usually travelled in family groups. Many were easy prey for guides who claimed to know the way in and out of the refugee camp, but who would end up robbing them, or leading them straight to the border patrol officers. Sometimes they would even be taken to the Khmer Rouge camp. There were also land mines in the jungle and if you didn't know the route, it was easy to find yourself in real trouble.

Eventually, Grandma gave Eng-Meng the nod and let him escort Aunt Hun and Heng to the refugee camp in Thailand. We all went to see Aunt Hun and Heng off at the station. They left for the refugee camp at the beginning of the monsoon, but by the end of the season we still hadn't heard any news from them. Eng-Meng had not returned to Phnom Penh to deliver any news, and we had no way of knowing that because of the influx of refugees the borders had now been closed. It was nearly four months after their departure that we finally had a letter from Aunt Hun telling Grandma that they had reached the camp. Eng-Meng and his family had been resettled in Australia, though, meaning the two girls were alone.

Grandma began to wonder what she could do. It was now difficult to cross the Thai border. Even if you bribed the guards, there was still a long jungle walk across the Chonburi mountain range to reach the camp.

Once again Grandma took me with her to Battambang, wanting to find out more. This time we went by boat. We didn't get very far, however, because fighting between the Khmer Rouge and the Vietnamese had flared up again and the roads were blocked. We returned home, but as soon as the route north was re-opened Grandma was anxious to set out again. She and Aunt Muy had found some gold inside an abandoned house, so her plans changed. This was to be a one-way trip and she hired her own people smugglers, paying them an ounce of gold per adult and half an ounce per child. We wanted to accompany them, but my family couldn't afford to pay for our escape. My new little brother, Heang, was less than a year old so it was also hard for Mama to travel. Grandma wanted me to go with them. I spent some time talking to Mama and Father about it. Naturally they were worried about me, but Father had always been a bit of a risk taker himself, and he encouraged me to go. With their support, I broke open my savings jar. I had enough gold pieces in it from my business to pay for the journey. We made a deal with the smugglers that I would pay half the fee up front, and the rest once my family knew I was safe in the camp. Mama was quiet before I left. I was excited, this was a leap of faith into safety and, hopefully, prosperity. I would be reborn, have a second chance of life, and find a promise of hope. I didn't know where my final destination would be, only that I had to make it to the refugee camp first. Father hoped against hope that I would find my freedom and happiness in a land of opportunities. Before I left he took me aside and gave me the best advice he knew; the one he missed five years ago: *America*. Father squatted down with one of his knees on the ground, in a position where his eyes were level with mine. It was the first time in my life where I looked right into my father's eyes as he leaned toward me and whispered his instruction softly and clearly into my ears.

"Huy, whatever happens, you need to look for a white flag with a red cross in the middle of it. You walk up to the people there, and tell them that you're lost. Tell them you are all alone. You're an orphan and you want them to take you to America." Father looked around, as if he was concerned people could overhear us, and then he continued, "Don't tell them you have parents alive in Phnom Penh - they'll send you back. Use your English. Just make sure you cross that border, either with or without Grandma. Do you understand? If they can't make it, don't worry about them but make sure you make it across yourself."

It was, I suppose, wicked advice, but it was a father's concern for his son above all else. He hardly spoke to anyone anymore, the treatment he had undergone at the hands of the Khmer Rouge had left him nearly speechless. He was now a man of few words, so having him talk to me like this had a profound effect on me and I vowed to follow his advice.

It was different for Mama. She didn't want me to go. She kept repeating, "He's too small, he's too young." She had not been able to say this when I had been taken away by Angkar, but now there was choice involved she was clearly very upset. Even when Angkar had taken me away to the Boys' Camp, at least she had had some idea of where I was, sometimes quite close to her. This time, I was going to another country, eventually overseas. As well as the potential dangers along the way, she was concerned that Grandma and my aunts would not look after me properly. She had seen us all survive under the Khmer Rouge, but now the family was going to be separated once more - perhaps forever. We might never see each other again. It is always easier for the one who is leaving and harder for those staying behind. Despite Mama's sadness, I was still very excited. Mama eventually realised that, I was capable of looking after myself if necessary. I had endured the Boys' Labour Camp, after all. Perhaps I would live through this adventure, too. This was neither a journey to a camp nor a return to a ghost city. This was a journey to freedom - if I stayed alive. Unlike the Khmer Rouge's broken promise, *tomorrow never came,* this was my journey to a new tomorrow.

Chapter Eighteen

The Great Escape

It was mid-October, 1980. I knew I had to travel as light as possible - I had no way of knowing just how long the journey would take. I only took a spare set of trousers, a couple of old shirts, my *Krama*, a nylon sleeping hammock and a few loose scraps of gold. I also had Aunt Hun's name written in English on a piece of cloth sewn inside the collar of my orange checked shirt. My gold was wrapped in a tiny envelope cut from an old plastic bag and tied up with a rubber band inside the hem of my shirt. Whatever happened I could not remove this shirt, not to sleep and not to wash, no matter how greasy or sweaty or stained it became. I had to wear it until I reached the safety of the distant camp.

Around midday, a dirty old army truck came to a sudden stop in front of our hut, going *clung clung* as its tyres hit the curb. It hissed loudly as the brakes were applied, and its muddy wheels looked like it had just emerged from the jungle. Two men stepped down - our people smugglers. One of them, the leader, Boo Sarith (Uncle Sarith), came over to collect his part payment. We had to complete the transaction quickly to avoid suspicion. Grandma had paid some already and had the rest with her, planning to pay the balance when they got to the camp safely. These were genuine people smugglers, they weren't concerned about this kind of arrangement. They'd already made a lot of money guiding people over the border.

I was ready to jump into the truck, but before I could Mama squatted down and hugged me to her chest for the longest time. I thought she would never let me go. She was crying, but didn't say a word and I knew she was thinking that this could be the last time she ever saw me. I vowed to myself that I would make it, and that my freedom would be repayment for the cost to her heart. Eventually she let go, and I said goodbye to the rest of my family. I climbed onto the back of the truck, which was fully loaded with rice as well as Grandma, Aunt Muy and her children, Chou (the only son of Small Uncle and Keang to survive the Khmer Rouge) and another family of five who had already been picked up.

I think Grandma wanted me there because she could rely on me if the situation demanded it. Mama believed Grandma only wanted me there as potential ransom, which would force Father to pay extra gold to the smugglers if necessary. I held on tied to my precious belongings, the *Krama* pouch, and took one last look at my family before I gradually slid down between those bags of rice convoy towards the north-west region of Cambodia. My younger brother, Huang, who was still too young to understand the situation, stood between Mama and Father silently as I tried to telegraph him my thought: "*I'll miss you. When I'm not here, you're now the eldest in the family and I will leave that older brother's duties to you. Take care of everyone while I am away.*" Mama wiped her nose and held back her tears as the truck slowly moved away, taking me with it.

The truck travelled north along Highway 5, zig-zagging around potholes and stopping for the many military checkpoints along the way. Every time we approached one we were told to stay beneath the cover so the guards couldn't see us. Sarith would go down and chat to the troops at the barricade, shaking their hands and offering smiles all around. Then we'd be on our way once more. Of course, the guards knew there were escapees in the truck and that the handshake was not an ordinary handshake - they were a way of transferring the bribes necessary for us to continue our journey. We finally arrived at Sisophon, the last town in the Cambodian northwest, late in the evening. This was as far as the truck could go - the rest of the journey was on foot. We were given shelter in an old hut for the night, but we ended up staying there for a few days because of a clash between the Vietnamese and the Khmer Rouge. Not knowing how long the trouble would continue, Sarith suggested we return to Battambang to wait it out. Grandma would have none of it, and insisted we stayed where we were. She wanted to be able to cross the border as soon as the fighting stopped. The monsoon was soon to end, but for now it was raining heavily.

After about three days there was no more gunfire, so after a quick breakfast we set out towards New Camp. This was the last and largest refugee camp inside Cambodia, and the final stop before KID about eight kilometres into Thailand. We were instructed not to travel together as a group, and had to walk separately, scattered along the muddy road. There were many others moving to and from New Camp, so we easily blended in. In good conditions, it would have taken us half a day, but these were far from good conditions. The rain had washed part of the road away, pot holes abounded and it was very slippery. Some sections were flooded up to my knees. When I finally reached New Camp, I was feeling tired but excited: freedom was finally within reach. I could see it in the shadow of the distant mountains. Sarith found us accommodation in a hut belonging to one of his relatives. We were told we should rest here for a few days waiting for the moon to wane - he said only when it was completely dark could we cross the border. Of course, this did not suit Grandma, nor the father of the other family we were travelling with. They wanted to leave immediately, and became very anxious and impatient. They insisted on setting out as soon as possible. Eventually Sarith agreed and said we could sneak out of the camp the next evening. We had dinner and then, nervous and excited, we started walking towards the border. We presumed more money must have changed hands, because we were told to assume the guards were all blind. We were told to wander through the bush individually as if we were looking for something. Once we were on the other side of the border we were to re-group and wait for our smugglers to arrive. They would wait behind a little, I guess in case there was trouble. We didn't get very far. The family of five were caught about a hundred metres along the road. I could see one of the guards talking to the father, presumably asking if anyone else was with him. Suddenly he fired shots in the air and yelled at us to reveal ourselves. Frightened by the gunfire, one by one we emerged from the trees. I walked toward the guards with my hands raised up high.

The guards rounded us up and took us to the general's office in New Camp. They lined us up with our backs against a wall of palm leaves. This wasn't exciting, this was frightening. We had no idea what would happen to us. While we stood there two guards searched us, warning us that if they found any gold or money it would be confiscated. We knew that if they couldn't find any they might keep us as prisoners until we revealed where we had hidden it, or maybe demand a ransom from our families. Even when they strip searched the women I knew they wouldn't find anything, as they had secreted their gold internally. A guard approached me and looked inside my *Krama*. He threw it to the ground and moved on. While I was waiting to be body searched by the next guard I managed to get the gold inside the hem of my shirt and drop it into the *Krama*. At the same time, we kept telling the guards that we had paid all our money to the people smugglers in Phnom Penh, and that we did not have anything left.

The general walked in then, and began shouting.

"Where are you going? Are you trying to escape to Thailand?"

We had planned our response, and told him that we were traders going to buy things to sell in Phnom Penh. This was hardly convincing, an old lady and some kids walking along a dangerous road at night across a border to buy goods! We were doomed. We had no idea what they were going to do with us when they found out we couldn't pay their ransom. We were held at gunpoint, and our smugglers were nowhere to be seen. We had been advised in no uncertain terms that if we were caught we were not to identify them. I wondered if the whole thing had been a set up. The other family was also very nervous. The general went into his office at the back of the hut, where there were chairs and a table. As he sat down, he said, "Don't lie to me. I know you're all trying to escape to Thailand!" It was pretty obvious we weren't traders.

Grandma followed him into his office in an attempt to beg

for mercy. She explained how we weren't really traders, but that we were looking for her daughters who had crossed the border a few months previously and hadn't been heard of since. As a mother, she was naturally worried. The hut was dimly lighted up with an oil lamp and I could only see their shadows. Then, a miracle occurred. I heard her initial pleading tones change, suddenly she became quite relaxed. She no longer used the very polite words to beg the general. Later, we would say to people that Grandma had paid her ransom years ago. She realised she knew the general from the old days at Kandal Market. He had been a beggar, sometimes coming to Grandma's stall for a handout. It was karma: what goes around comes around, as they say. As soon as he recognised her the general was a changed man and he ordered the guards to release us.

It wasn't a complete victory - he advised Grandma not to go into Thailand, explaining that gun battles were still frequent, and that Khmer Rouge militants and land mines were everywhere. Of course, we had heard these warnings before, and they didn't dissuade us. We went back to New Camp and found our smugglers in the hut we had stayed in the previous night. We decided to wait a few nights until there was no moon when it would be completely black.

Remembering Father's advice, the next morning I walked around the camp looking for a white flag with a red cross on it. It didn't take me long to find one. There were some foreigners working there. I was with my cousin Chou.

I stood outside the door of the Red Cross office and a woman came and asked what we were doing there. I replied with the words Father had told me to say.

"I'm lost. We're alone, just him and me. We don't know where our parents are," I lied, telling the officer that I had an aunt in KID and that we needed to go to her. She was impressed I could speak English. Another officer arrived to take a look at us. They wrote down Aunt Hun's name and told us to wait while they communicated with KID. Chou and I went back to the hut, checking to see we weren't being followed. I didn't want them to know I had lied. Before I had a chance to find out if they could help me, however, Sarith decided it was time to move.

While I had been away it had been decided that we were going to try for KID later that next night. The conditions were better, and instead of crossing the border near the checkpoint this time we were going to do it the hard way - through the jungle. The last time they had hoped to sneak us past the checkpoint because there were so many kids with us, but this time we were going to follow the tracks of so many refugees who had gone before us. There was no shortcut.

As night fell it soon became apparent these were perfect conditions - partly cloudy and no sign of the moon. There were only eight kilometres to travel, but they would be a hard eight kilometres, however at the other end lay both freedom and hope. We walked to a place far away from the checkpoint. In the distance the huge shadow of the mountains showed us where we were heading. All we had to do was find the camp beyond them. A lot of people went over the top and down the other side, but Sarith decided, possibly because of Grandma and the kids, that we would go around it. It would take longer, but it would be easier than climbing. There were fifteen of us in all, and Chou was the youngest and smallest. Grandma had promised the smugglers extra money if they piggybacked him. This will sound horrible, but to keep him quiet they made him smoke a lot of cigarettes with the hope he would sleep for the whole trip.

Once we were in the jungle it was pitch black. We tried to hold onto the shirt or the *Krama* of the person ahead of us. Sarith was at the front, the other smuggler was in the rear to make sure none of us got left behind. I soon had no sense of direction at all - they could have been taking us anywhere. The darkness was aiding our escape, but I could barely see a couple of metres in front of me. I followed the sounds of the footsteps in front and tried to keep hold of the shirt. It felt like we had been walking a long, long time, and I was becoming very tired, but knew I dared not have a break. I could only stop when I was told to stop. It was hard going through the scrub;

the foliage was often taller than I was. Sometimes I had to run to catch up. It was hard for my cousins as well and we knew it was dangerous.

Sometimes we would have to wait while Sarith surveyed the route ahead. I was grateful for the chance to rest. As well as the land mines and the Khmer Rouge, in some places, perhaps where mines had exploded, deep holes in the ground were flooded from the recent rain. I fell into one and struggled to get out, finally being rescued by one of the smugglers. There were swollen creeks to cross as well, and while the adults could leap across them we, kids, had to wade through deep water. We walked on and on, and I started to think we were travelling in circles. Surely, we must be at the camp by now? Occasionally I caught a glimpse of a campfire in the distance, or heard a faint noise. We were told this was a Khmer Rouge camp - we were circling around, trying to find a way past it.

We continued walking, but after about six hours I was exhausted. My legs were dragging and I was taking smaller and smaller steps. We had to find the camp before dawn or risk being caught. We might not be so lucky if we were captured again. Finally, after what seemed an eternity, we caught a glimpse of lights in front of us. All I could do was focus on those lights. The camp was not very far ahead. We struggled on a bit longer, and it wasn't far from dawn when we finally arrived near the entrance. Everyone was asleep inside, and I wondered if Aunt Hun was there, too, with no idea we were now so close to her. We had to get in before sunrise, but the camp was heavily guarded by the Thai army, and was surrounded by two barbed wire fences either side of a three-metre-wide red dirt road. It was lit with dim light bulbs every few hundred metres and Thai soldiers made regular jeep patrols along the road. Our smugglers considered bribing a guard on a checkpoint, but there were so many of us we knew it wouldn't be cheap - and there was no guarantee once the transaction had been conducted that we could trust them. They could take all our money and then still arrest us. And if the negotiations didn't go well they would know there were people hiding nearby trying to get inside. There was a strong chance we might all be shot.

We had heard stories of brutality undergone by refugees in the hands of the Thai military - young women being raped, men being kicked with hard soldier's boots until they coughed up blood. At the very least we would be robbed. Then if we survived that, we'd be driven to the top of the Dangrek mountain range. Our only option would be to walk down back towards the Cambodian border through a region notoriously thick with Khmer Rouge.

The risk was too high, so Sarith decided that we should try the only other alternative - sneaking through the barbed wire fences, one by one. I was still in hell, but I was nearly in heaven - if only I made it inside.

I was hanging back in the trees, hoping desperately that if a patrol came along I would not be seen. Sarith crossed the road and melted into the dark, while the other smuggler stayed with us. Because there was enough illumination from the dim perimeter light they used hand signals to let us know when it was safe to run to the other side of the road. Just as we were about to start crossing the headlights of a jeep came around the corner, shining right in our direction. The smuggler on our side frantically whispered to us, "Lie down, lie down!" We lay flat, our faces in the dirt. One soldier drove, the other was keeping a lookout. There were so many of us it was impossible we wouldn't be seen. My heart was beating like a drum. Surely the soldiers could hear it over the noise of the engine? They approached the place we lay and kept driving. Somehow, they had missed us!

We waited patiently until the jeep was out of sight, leaving behind a trail of red dust. I hadn't felt so much fear since the times I had sneaked into Phnom Penh at night. With the passing of the jeep I began to feel both excited and amazed. How had I made it this far? In just a few minutes it would all be over. I was so tired. I was exhausted, out of breath and besides my thumping heartbeat, all I could hear was my father's voice in my head, "Get into that camp with or without the rest of the group, you understand? If they don't make it, you keep going without them. You just make sure you make it into the camp."

I knew I had to get through those fences before the patrol came back, whether it was with Grandma and my cousins or without them. It might have been selfish but my freedom was too close and all I could think of was that once I made it a few more short metres, I was practically in America already.

Chapter Nineteen

Life in Khao-I-Dang Refugee Camp

The refugee camp in Thailand formally recognised by the international authorities known as Khao-I-Dang (KID) Camp was in Prachinburi province, approximately twenty kilometres north of Aranyaprathet, a well-known trading centre. It was the oldest and largest camp on the border and covered an area of over two square kilometres. Since it had opened at the end of 1979, as many as two thousand people a day had come there on a journey to a new life. By the time it closed its gates to new arrivals - before we arrived - the refugee population had grown to over 150,000. Refugees were housed in sections, with the ethnic Chinese in Section 17. Small huts ran in back to back rows from one side of the perimeter fence to the other. They were the same huts I was now so familiar with: bamboo frames and floors, palm leaf walls and straw roofs. Each hut had a bamboo sleeping section elevated just off the ground.

We had finally made it into the camp. It had been nerve wracking, but without incident. Once the jeep had gone past, the smugglers had pulled the barbed wire as wide as possible and one by one we crossed the road. I was very nervous when it was my turn, and took a deep breath as I waited for the smuggler's signal. When I heard him, I put my head low and ran as fast as I could. When I got to the fence I rolled under the lowest strand of wire into the camp, and the smuggler showed me where to hide until everyone else had made it. He then took us to his hut to stay for the night. Perhaps I thought I would be more excited: we had made it! We had made it to the camp! But I was so tired I just lay down, and quickly fell asleep, still in my wet clothes from the walk through the jungle.

I woke up the next morning and realised, as the sleep fell from my eyes, that I was at last inside the camp. I needed to find Aunt Hun and Heng. We were in a Khmer section, so I started to walk around as soon as we'd had breakfast. I had

Aunt Hun's address, didn't take me long to find her. She was just coming out of her hut to get something to eat when she saw me walking towards her. I told her we had arrived last night.

"How did you get here? Are you by yourself?" she asked.

"We hired a smuggler. There's Grandma, Aunt Muy and her children and Chou."

"Where are they now?"

"With the Khmers. We slept at the smuggler's place last night."

She told me to bring Grandma to her as soon as possible.

I went back to the others and Sarith came with us back to Section 17. It was now time to finalise my debt. I had arranged for my parents to pay him the balance of our agreement when he returned to Phnom Penh. As well as advice, there was one piece of insurance my father had given me just before I climbed onto the truck to leave for the refugee camp. He had taken out a riel note and torn it in two. He had given me one half, and kept the other.

"When you're safely inside the camp give your half to the smuggler and tell him to bring it back to me so we know you're alive," he had warned me. "I'll only pay him when I see it again. Keep it with you at all times and never let anyone know you have it."

As I still couldn't read or write, this was the only way we could communicate. As well as the note, I also gave Sarith my sleeping hammock to take back to the city.

After we finally settled in at Aunt Hun's hut, many of her neighbours came to welcome us. They were amazed by us: a sixty-year-old grandmother, one widow and six children, the eldest - me - just fifteen years old but look as little as a ten-year-old boy. There was confusion because I had contacted the Red Cross in New Camp. The Red Cross woman had actually come to Section 17 the day before to find Aunt Hun and ask her about me - Aunt Hun had realised who I was but had no idea about Chou. People began to wonder who this mysterious boy could be, they rarely had officials visiting them.

One by one the neighbours came over to greet us. They

shook their heads as they heard Grandma's story about the general at New Camp. We found out that our border crossing experience was little different to anyone else's. It was only those in the very early days who had made it here on UNHCR trucks or by walking along the road and through the front gate. Everyone else had either walked around the mountain like us or gone over it. Everyone agreed it was a miracle we had made it. Grandma was admired for her courage and dedication at such an old age. Chou was only four. And I was a boy who not only spoke English, but had managed to get a Red Cross official to visit their section of the camp. We were almost famous! It was then I heard that the Red Cross woman had told Aunt Hun she would bring me and Chou back with her on her next trip - we really could have arrived in the camp in style rather than running at night through the jungle risking life and limb.

    Aunt Hun had been very worried about me. She didn't know if I was really alone in New Camp or not. She said she had even attempted to hire someone to go and get me, but the guide had asked for six thousand baht (US$300) for the pair of us. The average wage of the volunteer workers in the camp was about 300 baht a month, so this was the equivalent of more than a year's wages! Aunt Hun made some money giving French and English lessons to children, but had nowhere near the amount required to save me. She was very relieved when we arrived safely under our own steam.

    I was excited to be in the camp, but the reality of our situation soon hit home. The camp was officially closed to new arrivals and no one knew what to do with so many refugees - the wait for visas was long. There were on again off again decisions by the Thai government and the UNHCR as to what they should do. Some people were even being voluntarily repatriated to Cambodia. We soon learned that we were not going to be considered official refugees. IDs would not be issued to us. Because we weren't recognised we weren't given a food ration. More importantly, it meant we couldn't apply for resettlement. Our visa applications would not be processed.

We had risked our lives and spent so much money coming all this way, and for what?

I wondered if I would have been better off staying in Phnom Penh fixing bicycles. There I was busy, I had an income. Here I had no food and no work. It was boring not having anything to do. To make matters worse Aunt Hun and Heng's names appeared on the UNHCR notice board just five days after we arrived. The French Embassy in Bangkok had approved their sponsorship by a professor, Madame Charriere, for resettlement in France after just a short interview. I was surprised to learn that they were going to France and not America. At least Grandma's nephew and his family were living in the States, as far as I knew we had no one in France.

It turned out that it was actually because of my parents that Aunt Hun and Heng were going to Europe. Aunt Hun had finished 5th grade at a Chinese primary school around the time I was born, but had to leave when Grandfather Lee couldn't afford the school fees. Father asked Aunt Hun to help look after me while Mama prepared sweets for next day's market stall. She sat around at home playing musical instruments and reading Chinese comic books until Father, with his Khmer ID, managed to obtain one for Aunt Hun as well. Mama used her connection with the principal of the school she sold shaved ice at so that Aunt Hun was eventually able to attend the Pochentong Khmer school. After this she then went on to university, where she had been taught French by Madam Charriere up until the arrival of the Khmer Rouge. While she was in Vietnam seeking sponsorship to go to America she had used the Red Cross to find contact details of her old lecturer, and had sent her a letter.

After Aunt Hun had arrived at KID, she had managed to ask for sponsorship from Madam Charriere and had even written to the ambassador explaining the urgency of her request and asking for priority processing. Amazingly the French official, Monsieur Tricorno, had come to the camp and called her in for an interview. As she entered the room, she saw he was holding her Aerogramme. The first question he asked was, "*Avez-vous écrit cette lettre vous-même?*" (Did you write this letter yourself?)

"*Oui, j'ai écrit cette letter moi-même?*" (Yes, I did.) Aunt Hun told him.

"There were a few mistakes," Monsieur Tricorno said.

"I know there were," Aunt Hun said, "but I wasn't so concerned about them as long as you got my message."

After a short pause, Monsieur Tricorno chuckled and told her, "Go and have some passport photos taken."

Aunt Hun didn't understand what he meant: was this acceptance or rejection? She must have looked confused because Monsieur Tricorno repeated himself, and also used his fingers to indicate the shape of a small picture frame.

She walked back to her hut still stunned. All her Section 17 neighbours were curious to hear what had happened. "I don't know if I'm going. He told me to have some passport photos ready." People who had been in the camp for a while knew that this meant she had been accepted. I don't know which adage explains what happened to Aunt Hun, either "the pen is mightier than the sword" or "actions speak louder than words," but whichever it was, it was clear that her little letter had touched Monsieur Tricorno's heart.

Within a week, Aunt Hun and Heng were going to be sent to a camp further inside Thailand for processing before being sent to Paris. Without them the rest of us were screwed. Aunt Hun was the smartest of her brothers and sisters, so she now put on her thinking cap trying to figure out a way she could take the rest of us with her. They had applied for two people to go; now there were eight more of us! She spoke to the UNHCR, telling them about how more members of her family had just arrived. The officer felt that one or two people might be able to accompany her and Heng, but not more than that. A large number would in all likelihood prevent Aunt Hun herself from leaving - especially as we weren't official refugees. If she waited with all of us it could be years before all our applications were approved. With this in mind, Aunt Hun thought hard, and eventually came to a decision.

She took me to meet one of the Thai officials, a man named Mr Anuxon. Aunt Hun had actually been offered a job with him, but because she was leaving she hadn't taken it. It was risky to take an unregistered refugee to the office, but she felt this was the only chance we had.

"Can you help my nephew? Can you give him a job? And can you do something about his status?" she asked.

Mr Anuxon replied vaguely that he would try.

On the morning of November 11, 1980, the feelings of excitement I had once known had turned resolutely into anxiety. We all went to the bus terminal just outside the camp's main gate to send Aunt Hun and Heng on their way. Aunt Hun's students were there, as were other neighbours and friends. There were other refugees leaving, too, so there was quite a crowd.

For those who were departing their hearts were filled with hope and excitement, while those who were staying behind were left wondering when it would be their turn. I wondered what would happen to me. I still hoped Aunt Hun would take me with her. The UNHCR official started calling out the names of the people who were getting on the bus. He called Aunt Hun and Heng - and then Grandma and Chou. Aunt Hun was taking the oldest and youngest of us with her. I suppose I was the smart nephew who was in some ways disposable - and who would also be a help for Muy and her children. I couldn't help feeling upset as I watched them climb on board the bus; despite Aunt Hun's promises that she would try and do something for us as soon as she arrived at the next camp.

Once Aunt Hun and Heng had left, Aunt Muy, her children and I were given permission to stay in her old hut and our neighbours were kind enough to share their limited food ration with us. We were given rice, soy beans and dried yellowtail fish which would only last us a few weeks. Despite the UNHCR paying the Thai government to house us, the food was very poor. The fish, *Pratoo* in Thai, was horrible. It came in bags that were old and long past their expiry date. The *Pratoo* were yellow and smelled of fish oil and no matter how many times they were washed they tasted salty. The Section 17 team leader, an elderly Chinese man who was responsible for going to the UN holding centre to collect his group's food ration generously offered some to us. It was very kind of him to do this - these people had so little already. We were all survivors of the Khmer Rouge, though, and because we had all endured the same depravation they understood our situation. As well as the ration, they would occasionally be given pork or chicken, and this kind man would chop off a piece of meat from each household's entitlement to make up a small portion for us. Apart from that, though, we had the disgusting salted *Pratoo* every day. I ended up arguing with Aunt Muy about the food. When hunger comes in the door, love for a hungry nephew flies out the window, especially when you have four starving young mouths of your own to feed. I couldn't blame Muy too harshly - she had suffered greatly during the regime; her husband had died and now she was bringing up their children alone. Her eldest was just a year or so younger than me. I didn't really know her very well - even in Phnom Penh we had not spent much time together. She had not wanted Father to marry Mama, and it was Muy who had gone into competition with Mama at the market. Despite my complaints, I was still grateful to her for cooking and looking after me. It can't have been easy with four demanding children of her own.

I was finding the situation very difficult, living like a beggar in a refugee camp, far worse than those in the streets on Phnom Penh. I had no official status, no food ration, no work, no school and no hope of getting out. Even my gold had gone. I had worked so hard for it, and been through so much to bring it into the camp. Aunt Hun had asked me if I had anything valuable with me. I pulled out the gold from my orange checked shirt and handed it to her. Aunt Hun told me she would look after it but I had never seen it again - as she had given it to Muy to buy food with.

If I could find a sponsor I would have some chance of leaving. Grandma's older brother in California had a daughter I knew from the days we had spent time looking after Great

Grandmother. I wrote to her begging for sponsorship and money. She very generously sent me a cheque for US$50, but was unable to sponsor me as she wasn't yet a US citizen. This was my last hope of emigrating to America, my dreams were shattered, and my road to freedom was blocked before I had had a chance to start upon it. I knew that if I couldn't secure a visa that at some stage I might be forced back to Cambodia and all my efforts to get this far would have been wasted. As Muy was responsible for the food, I gave her the $50.

On the positive side, I started making friends with the neighbours. It was easy as I was still famous as the boy who had brought the Red Cross official. I set up an informal English class, teaching my cousins and any other kid who was interested. Sometimes their parents would offer me food in exchange. I became very close to the children of the Chan family who lived in the hut opposite us, especially one of their daughters, who was also called Muy. She was a year or two older than me, and although the youngest she was known as Mom. Her father reminded me of my Chinese grandfather: tall and thin and a man of few words. I didn't know if he spoke Khmer, as the little I heard him say was in Chinese. Mom's mother was much friendlier. They were stuck in limbo as well - there were seven of them in total, the parents and two boys and three girls. Mom had other brothers and sisters in France and America who would send them money so they could buy extra food from the camp market.

Apart from what I could scrape up by teaching English, I had no savings and no hope of a job that would bring in extra money. All I had were soy beans and that damn *Pratoo*.

Mom started teaching me French in case I emigrated to France with Aunt Hun. I had now missed five years of school. Even when I had attended, French wasn't an option in the school I was enrolled in. There was no formal education as such inside the camp, although if you had enough money, like Mom's family, you could send your children for private lessons. Sometimes I would wait outside the hut where the kids were being taught, hoping to hear something. Every time the teacher saw me, however, he'd slam the window shut. I was grateful Mom shared her French with me.

    In the middle of the camp was a space where Thai traders had set up a small market. They would arrive every morning to sell farm produce and other goods. I had to do something, so I sometimes woke early to see if any of the stallholders needed help. When I couldn't find anything after a few days I went to the UNHCR office and asked Mr Anuxon if he had work for me. He allowed me to volunteer as an interpreter for the UNHCR workers distributing food. Although it paid no money, it allowed me to practice my English and to start learning a new language: Thai. I had no set hours, but had to be there before food distribution began because this was the busiest part of the day. As there were so many refugees the process often went on into the afternoon. Although I wasn't paid, I was offered food - and no *Pratoo*! I was given the same meals as the official Thai staff. Because I didn't have anything for breakfast I was usually starving by the time lunch was served. In the evenings, I would sometimes wait near Mom's hut hoping they would invite me to dinner, which they usually did. Because of the money coming to them from overseas they also ate well. One night when I was helping myself to some meat, one of Mom's brothers joked that I would never grow taller if I didn't eat my vegetables. I was still very short, but nothing could keep me from that meat.

    Because of the generosity of our neighbours and the kindness of the UNHCR staff the hunger pangs gradually began to fade. Every morning I would head up to the office looking for something to do, and also hoping that the registration lists had been re-opened, although every morning the answer was the same. At the end of the day Mr Anuxon sometimes gave me a tin of sardines or some soy beans to take home to Muy or the neighbours. Sardines were valuable - you could trade with a can of sardines as they were not part of the official ration. Sometimes, too, tins of tuna in tomato sauce would appear in the office and this was a delicacy as well - when compared to beans and *Pratoo*! I enjoyed going to the office -

it got me out of the hut and helped me stay busy, and now Aunt Muy and her children didn't have to worry about food as much. I guess Aunt Hun was right in leaving me here to look after her sister and my cousins. The volunteer work had in one sense turned into a paid job. It couldn't have come sooner - our original supply of food from the neighbours was nearly all gone.

CHAPTER TWENTY

FREEDOM CAME AT A PRICE

It was often chaos in the UNHCR office as refugees waited for interviews with the diplomatic representatives of various nations. As soon as they heard that someone had arrived to review applications and requests, crowds would magically appear. Everyone wanted to get out of the rotten camp and they knew there were only limited opportunities to have their voices heard. The French Ambassador[7], Monsieur Tricorno, was a very grumpy man. He would charge past all those who were waiting and screaming out, *"Excusez-moi, excusez-moi s'il vous plait."* He'd get inside the office and slam a dossier onto to a desk. Without waiting to calm down he would have his interpreter look at the top of the pile of papers and call the first applicant's name. He'd assess their situation - and their family's - and make a decision to accept or reject their application based on the reasons they offered during the interview balanced against what they had said on their written application.

I was among those who would run to the office hoping for an interview, despite the fact that Muy and I never had a chance, because we didn't have an overseas sponsor. It didn't matter that our names weren't on the list, I would hang around up there, hoping without reason that a miracle would occur. Being there gave me a chance to hear news from our neighbours as they exited their interviews. We were all at the mercy of Monsieur Tricorno. Some people would go into his office and come out despondent, a REJECTED stamp on the back of their photo ID. Someone came up with an idea of a way to get around this. The ID card was just a Polaroid photo of them holding an A4-sized blackboard with their name and

---

7 He wasn't the actual ambassador of France, but in the camp, we called all the diplomatic representatives 'ambassador'.

identification number written on it. My friend simply licked off the stamp as soon as he left the office, wiping the rest of it off with the back of his hand while the ink was still wet. Because Monsieur Tricorno was so busy he did not keep records of his interviews or a list of who had been rejected, only those who were accepted. The only thing to show the status of your interview was the stamp on the back of the photo. My friend said he had been rejected three times. It was impossible for Monsieur Tricorno to remember everyone's faces, he saw so many people - and names were difficult as well as there were so many similar pronunciations.

We were all wary of his mood. If he was very grumpy - perhaps he had had a bad trip from Bangkok - it seemed like he would reject many applicants. He would only come one morning a week, so if you missed out on an interview it felt like forever until your next chance. A week in KID was a long time. For those who were lucky and had ACCEPTED stamped onto their photos, there was still a delay - some families waited weeks until they saw their names posted on the notice board giving a date of departure. This was where you wanted to read your name - it was a ticket, not just to France, but to any country accepting refugees. It was a ticket to your new life.

Beside the frenzy of the UNHCR office and my volunteer work, there was not much to do in the camp except talk. Some evenings the UN would bring in a van with a projector and screen Western movies on a big sheet. Because there was not much else to do, these occasions were always crowded. Sometimes you couldn't get in front of the sheet and had to watch from behind, meaning everything looked reversed. It was still better than no movie at all. A well-respected Khmer teacher who taught English at the camp sat in the van with a microphone and simultaneously translated for us. One movie had a character called Max. I liked that name, Max, Maximillian - Steve McQueen in "Nevada Smith." It had been five years since I had seen a movie, and I thought that Max was the actor's real name - I had forgotten the distinction between actors and characters.

There was no electricity in the huts. We used candles and oil lamps at night. It was dark and quiet, just the faint sounds of gentle conversation from people in their huts or under a street light. Sometimes we played seventies songs on a cassette player, hits like "San Francisco" or "Love You More Than I Can Say," or "Yesterday Once More." Time passed slowly, and these songs helped to ease the boredom and worry. Although I didn't quite understand the lyrics, they helped me get through that time. I wished it was yesterday once more, back in the days when I was a little kid at Kandal Market and my biggest concern was which song the radio would play next.

My favourite song in the camp, however, was not a popular hit, but a song in Khmer written about us:

From there to here, we carried only one tiny pouch,
There was no fear nor concern just the two of us, my dear
We've come to live together in a new land
We have plenty of food and there is no need for us to worry
Now in Khao-I-Dang, you've become pretentious,
You've forgotten me, your spouse
You've forgotten our time of sorrow
I love you, but you have a deceiving heart
You've forgotten the night we escaped across the fields and jungle

Suddenly now you've forgotten everything
You've forgotten the time of our dismay
My heart is broken and disappointed
I love you so much every night and day
I think and dream of only you in my sleep
Oh, my darling, please do not forget
When you've reached the West, don't forget the East
You can forget about me, but don't forget your birthplace
It's a rich and beautiful land; you'll return someday my dear

You've forgotten everything since 1975
We suffered and survived the revolution

I starved myself to feed you
I sacrificed all the food I had for you
Oh, my darling, please do not forget
Now you've lived in the West, don't forget the East
You can forget about me, but don't forget your country
It's a rich and beautiful land; you'll return someday my dear.

Although it couldn't compare to how much we'd suffered in the Khmer Rouge labour camps, the situation inside KID had its own moments of despair. We were surrounded by barbed wire and patrolling soldiers. If I stepped beyond the perimeter I could be sent straight back to Cambodia, possibly via a Khmer Rouge jungle camp. Some people had been in KID for more than a year - and they were official refugees. People were desperate to get out. They would fake their ID, claiming a relationship to a family they did not have. If they had money they would buy name and dates of birth so they could fit the profile of a dead brother or sister or child of a family who were further up the application hierarchy. Many hoped that once they had been resettled they could reverse the identification changes so they could sponsor their own families. As a result of these tactics, some families who had arrived in KID together were now separated once more. There was much sadness and unhappiness in the camp.

I wasn't immune from doctoring my ID. Grandfather's name was Lee, and I had been named Lee Huy. In her last days at KID, Aunt Hun had been frantic, making sure she knew our personal details for the application she hoped to make for us when she arrived at the next camp. She had talked to me about my name and my date of birth. She wanted to ensure my profile was consistent with what she would put and be as simple as possible for us both to memorise. Aunt Hun also told me to change my name, using Grandma's maiden name like she had, rather than the surname Lee. She didn't want to have to explain why I had a different surname to her. Thus, I became Do Huy instead of Lee Huy. (Chinese and many other Asian people have their surnames at the front). We felt it would fit in well with my story about being an orphan. Father's words still rang in my ears: "Tell them you are alone. You were separated from your parents and you don't know if they are dead or alive."

I really wanted to leave the camp and get resettled. Part of the reason was so that I could begin sponsoring the rest of my family. I was their only hope, and I knew that Father was relying on me. Even though I was the oldest grandson of the Lee family - a place of privilege in Chinese tradition - I agreed to register my name as Do Huy so that I became a closer relative to Aunt Hun and Grandma. Desperate times call for desperate measures

Aunt Hun had taken Do as a surname when she was in Vietnam - Grandma's brother who was in the US had this surname, and she felt it would help her get into America. "I also wrote to my French professor under this name. When I wrote to the French ambassador from the camp I also signed as Do Hun. We must be consistent, and not confuse them. If they are confused and asking questions about our names, we will be here forever."

Aunt Hun had even suggested she would change her surname to that of her old teacher to "express her gratitude" but this hadn't gone down well with Madam Charriere, as she didn't like the idea of altering names.

As for my date of birth, birthdays were different in Cambodia: we didn't celebrate with cake and presents. I didn't even know my date of birth, just that when Chinese New Year arrived that I was a year older. During our time under the Khmer Rouge we had not even known when it was New Year - like many people I had literally lost track of time. There were no records to say that my birthday was in November of a certain date or year. However, I remembered my Chinese zodiac sign is the Dragon[8]; even that I had no memory of what year it was. Grandfather Lee was very proud to have his first

---

8 Years later, I learned that Mama looked down at the end of the bed straining to see me when she heard me cry, the first exhalation of my baby lungs. The clock on the wall read 3:15 in the afternoon on Saturday November 14, 1964.

grandson born in the year of the dragon; a sign of great things to accompany me in my life. The one most important thing that had yet to materialise was my education. If I didn't know how to read and write, nothing would come true. It was taken away from me ten years ago. At sixteen, I understood in two years' time my school days would be over. Thus, Aunt Hun and I decided to roll back my age so that I would still have a chance to attend school for a few years in my new country. We picked a date at random, one we hoped was easy to remember. We settled on May 16, 1966: 5.16. Five plus one equalled six and that was the best I could do with mathematics. We had discussed using January the first, but felt it was too obvious.

Aunt Hun kept her promise to us. As soon as she arrived at the next camp she began writing letters on our behalf to the UNHCR requesting that we should all be reunited. I had no way of knowing this, of course, nor if she had been, or would ever be, successful. Aunt Muy and I waited day after day, week after week, checking the notice board every morning and hoping for a miracle. There were so many other people in the camp all anxious to see their names appear. People would scramble to the notice board as soon as a new list was posted. It wasn't just those like us who were waiting for an interview - even those who had been accepted for resettlement checked the board everyday hoping their departure date had been set. Some would stare at the board for hours as if this would make the words they wanted to see suddenly appear. They would check and re-check in case they had missed their name the first, the second or the third time.

Due to the crowd that would assemble I had trouble even seeing the papers when they were first put up. As I was little it was easy for me to duck underneath and burrow through people's legs, but that would only allow me to see the bottom of the page. I would have to wait a few minutes before everything settled down before I could see the whole thing.

Then, one morning, the miracle we had been hoping for, knowing only a miracle would help us, was there! As I was reading down from A to Z, I saw Aunt Muy's name, then those of her children - and then mine! Without having either an interview or official refugee status we were being transferred! I ran to tell Aunt Muy. She couldn't believe it, and ran to check the board. The neighbours were stunned as well. We had been hoping to meet the ambassador, perhaps obtain a change in our status, but this was beyond our wildest dreams. Muy returned from the notice board just as shocked as I was. She couldn't read well, but people confirmed her name was there.

We didn't know it then, but Aunt Hun had managed to arrange our transfer by becoming a proxy sponsor. Our new status certainly had the neighbours talking. First it had been Aunt Hun's relatively quick movement through the camp, then our arrival with the visit by the Red Cross, and now the transfer of a widow with four children and a young boy in less than three months. They were amazed. Some went to check for themselves, having been in the camp much longer than we had been. Sure enough, our names were there, with Aunt Hun as our sponsor: a refugee sponsoring another refugee! Some began to say we were queue jumpers, although there was no queue. They were upset because they had had interviews, they possessed ID cards - and they were still stuck in the damn camp. Mom and her brothers couldn't understand what had happened - they had been helping me out with food and now I was going to leave the camp before them. We didn't even have an actual sponsor - just a proxy sponsor! This was a miracle not just for Section 17 but for the whole camp. It was unprecedented. Perhaps Mom would have been more upset if she and the rest of the Chans hadn't already been accepted for resettlement, although they were still waiting to hear the date of their transfer.

Then, like déjà vu, just three days before we were due to leave who should appear in the camp but Small Uncle! I was having enough trouble trying to work out what was a dream and what was reality. I now knew how Aunt Hun had felt when we arrived, but I didn't want my uncle to feel what I had when Aunt Hun had left. I wondered if I could use my influence to take him and his wife, Keang, out with me. Neither of them could speak a word of English or Thai, and Bim (Chou's little sister) was just a toddler. I knew that if I left them there they had little chance of leaving the camp anytime soon. They didn't have official status either, and I couldn't say whether they would be as well looked after by the neighbours as we had been. Many of those neighbours would be gone soon, anyway, so I couldn't trust that they would have enough food to live on. It was imperative that I take them out with me - but how?

By this stage I had been working in the UNHCR office for a couple of months so I could speak Thai with some proficiency. My skill at interpreting Cambodian, Vietnamese and Chinese into Thai and English was well known in the office, and amongst the aid workers - in fact they were very impressed that although I was just a kid I could speak five different languages and swap from one to the next almost simultaneously. Most interpreters at the camp could only handle one or two. The officials were also fond of me because I was this small, skinny kid with no ID who was roaming around the camp and into the UN offices seemingly at will. I was well liked, and I made sure my Thai became quite fluent. I felt it would be important to be able to speak it well one day.

On the date of departure for the processing camp, I took Small Uncle and his family to the bus station with me. They had no permission to leave. We had had no approval from the French authorities nor the UNHCR. Mr Anuxon was not here. Although I would have liked to have said goodbye and thanked him, it was fortunate he was absent because of what I was able to do next. I was watching the Thai UNHCR officer closely as she checked people's names off against the list she had for departure to Phanat-Nikhom camp. I pulled my uncle close to me on my left. The officer was on my right. She had known me from the office, so she was prepared to listen as I explained that not only was Small Uncle part of my family, but he had a little son waiting for him up ahead. This was when it was good I could speak Thai - I wouldn't have had a chance of explaining this to her in any other language. I didn't think it was going to work, but she was a kind woman and suddenly, surprisingly, she nodded, and let all of us get on the bus. "Padi, Padi, Del Del", Get on, get on, hurry, hurry up!" she said. Despite the trouble, she might get into, she felt enough compassion for us that she turned a blind eye. That sort of kindness makes history - Small Uncle and his family must have set some kind of record, they had no ID and had only been in KID for three days! They were the luckiest Cambodians in Thailand. I wished I could help everyone. I wanted Mama and Father on the bus, my brothers, and Mom, too, who stood there sadly as I said goodbye. I promised I would write to her, and watched her waving as the bus pulled away.

Those of us on the bus had graduated from tragedy, and some us were now starting to study hope. For many who were left behind, however, the misery and not knowing continued. Some were faced with the prospect of never making it out at all and were expecting to be sent back to Cambodia. Others had bought fake IDs for family members and had watched them leave, hoping desperately they would be reunited one day. Despite pressure from the UN, the Thai government was attempting to close KID, and if this occurred, those remaining there faced a bleak future. The Khmer Rouge may have gone for now, but the terror of their potential return was ever present in every Cambodian. You don't live through that kind of brutality without it scarring your heart, your soul, your very being - possibly even more so if you are just a child. Was it so wrong to want to leave all this behind, to seek a new, safer, fairer, more hopeful life in a different country?

As the bus was took me away from the misery and barbed wire of KID I wondered whether, somewhere, somehow in the future, I could regain some of the time I had lost. Khao-I-Dang slowly disappeared behind me in the red dust. The bus engine roared, slowly transporting me to find my freedom, but I had that Khmer refugee song playing in my head, reminding me not to forget Cambodia and my experiences there, both good and bad. It was a song about family separation, families who had survived the Khmer Rouge, a song about escaping through the jungle, about finding temporary sanctuary in a refugee camp. I couldn't help myself and started sobbing, nearly choking on my own tears with thoughts of how fortunate I was. Unlike my father who had missed his opportunity to get onto that helicopter on April 12, 1975, I'd been given a ticket to freedom, but this freedom came at a price! I wondered what my parents, especially Father, waiting anxiously to hear from me back in the ruins of Phnom Penh, would think when they heard my news: *they might never see me again.*

Chapter Twenty One

To Paris or Not To Paris

It took hours before the bus finally arrived at our new camp in the Thai province of Chonburi. This was Phanat-Nikhom Camp. The centre was divided into two parts straddling the highway. On one side was the processing centre. Once you had your final interviews and made it through there, you progressed to the transit centre across the road. You needed all your paperwork completed before you made this short but important journey. In the transit centre, you went for a full medical examination and only once you and your family had passed this health check would you be sent for resettlement overseas.

I was so excited to have made it this far. As we approached I kept watching, waiting for my first glimpse of it. So far everything that had happened to me since I said goodbye to my parents had been dependant on my desire to leave Cambodia. Now that process was out of my hands - out of our hands. Our fate lay with the UNHCR. Aunt Hun was there to meet us - you can imagine her surprise when instead of six people, nine of us stepped off the bus. Chou couldn't believe that his parents and a new little sister, less than six months old, had somehow arrived out of the blue. Originally Aunt Hun had applied to take Heng with her to France. Then Grandma and Chou had been added, then Muy and her kids and me, finally Small Uncle, his wife and his little baby girl - we were now a grand total of lucky thirteen!

Along with the other fortunate refugees who were on the bus, we were escorted to the processing centre where we filled out registration forms and had our photos taken. Although Small Uncle and his family weren't on the official list, it didn't seem to matter - things were more informal here and we registered them quite easily. It was only near the end of the process that an official noticed we had no country to go to. As

Aunt Hun was our sponsor, not someone overseas, our final destination was listed as Phanat-Nikhom - for a family reunion.

"Where are you all going? Which country?" the UNHCR officer asked.

Aunt Hun and I looked at each other, lost for words. By this time the other refugees who had been on the bus with us had all moved on, while the other members of my family were away from the counter, unaware of what was going on. Every arrival at Phanat-Nikhom had a destination overseas, we didn't. We'd been allowed to come this far on the basis of Aunt Hun being reunited with her family, but she couldn't say we were going to France with her.

"What's your suggestion?" Aunt Hun asked the officer after a while. "What country could we apply for?"

There were workers and volunteers from many different nations who were compassionate to our cause, and they began to discuss our situation. Someone produced a list of potential countries. America was out of the question, we had no sponsor and they were now prioritising Vietnamese refugees. The United States of America felt they owed the people of Vietnam a favour because of their involvement in the Vietnam War, but Cambodia was simply a collateral damage. Japan had a good human rights record, but were currently only accepting single females because the government wanted to keep their Japanese race as pure as possible. Anyone who was non-Japanese was considered an alien. Given the size of our group, two families and a lonely boy, it would be futile applying there.

"Canada has a good refugee program," someone suggested.

"No way, Canada's too cold. Six months of freezing snow," someone else at the back called out. It was something to consider given how warm Cambodia was compared to Canada. New Zealand was also suggested, but before we could comment someone else shouted out.

"Why not try Australia? It's a big country and very friendly."

The officer who was helping us register agreed with the suggestion.

"Yes, Australia. Australia has a special humanitarian

program and it takes widows." I wasn't sure what to make of all the countries that had been mentioned, the only name I recognised was America. I couldn't have told you where any of the others were. We didn't have much choice, though, and so Australia was nominated as our ultimate destination. I was still not sure I would ever make it there. Yes, it accepted families and widows, but what about me? Would it take me as well? None of us had a sponsor there.

After all our paperwork was completed, we were assigned a place to stay in the block next to Aunt Hun and Heng. The building was like a warehouse, with walls made of cement board and a tin roof. We had a space approximately two and a half metres wide and five metres long. There were no interior walls, but each family hung up curtains at night so there was some privacy. In the day, we generally pulled them down, and you could see from one end of the building to the other. There were three other buildings like ours in a block of four, arranged so there was a central courtyard.

Once we had settled in, I learned how Small Uncle had made it to KID. After we had arrived in the refugee camp, Grandma Lee had sent him a letter. Because there was no postal service in Cambodia she had actually posted it to her relatives in Vietnam, and it had eventually been picked up by Father. Small Uncle had no idea when he set out for the camp that Aunt Hun, Heng, Grandma and his son, Chou, had already left KID. He hadn't used Boo Sarith but a different group of people smugglers and had travelled much the same route, the only difference being that his journey was more perilous due to increased activity from the Khmer Rouge. Small Uncle and Keang had spent some time discussing whether they should bring Bim with them, or leave her with Mama in Phnom Penh. Perhaps the thought of being separated from another child was too much for Keang, because she insisted that the family should stay together. Mama agreed, despite the protests of the *Nyak Noum Pluo* (people who lead the way) who were concerned Bim would cry when they cross the jungle at night and alert the Thai guide or Khmer Rouge to their presence. As it happened, she often cried during the journey to New Camp, and the smugglers even suggested abandoning her that evening when they were ready to cross the eight kilometres of jungle to get to KID. In the end, they gave Bim two sleeping pills. It was a nerve wracking decision. It was as good as abandoning her because there was no guarantee she would stay asleep, and there was also the danger she could overdose. As it was, she slept all the way to KID without harm.

Meanwhile, Aunt Hun was worried about the increased numbers and what impact this would have on our chances of resettlement. She felt that the right way to deal with the situation was to march straight into Monsieur Tricorno's office and confront him the next morning. In one hand, she held a card with four names on it - those who had been already accepted for France. In the other, she held another card with names of the remaining nine. She showed Monsieur Tricorno both sets.

"All these people are my family. I've been sponsored. When are we going to proceed? Are you accepting all thirteen of us to go to France?" she asked the surprised man.

Monsieur Tricorno glanced at the cards and said he knew nothing about the nine new arrivals.

"I will accept the first group of four only," he said. "Who are the others?"

"What do you mean by you don't know anything about them?" Aunt Hun confronted him. "If France hadn't accepted their sponsorship, how were they able to get onto the bus from KID to come here?"

The poor man looked confused. He left the room and went into the UNHCR office, perhaps to check on some paperwork. When he returned, he shook his head.

The excitement we had been feeling quickly dissipated when Aunt Hun returned. It seemed our hope of going to France had now disappeared. It wasn't going to be so easy - we had hoped to slip one past the ambassador but he had not fallen for it. Of course, he could not remember everyone he had interviewed, but presumably he had some sense of which people he had spoken to and which people he hadn't.

Another month passed without any further news. We still did not know where we would be sent, if anywhere. There was not much to do except wait. Back in KID, I had had a say in what happened, especially because of my language skills, but here I left everything to Aunt Hun. While wandering around the camp one morning I managed to find a job at the market. At least this took my mind off our predicament. Once again, it was my multilingual ability that assisted me - a Thai clothes seller enlisted me as a sales assistant. I was good because I could translate the needs of the refugees for his Thai staff. It wasn't a normal market - the stall holders weren't allowed inside, so they set up their shops near the fence and passed their goods through the barbed wire. I was paid fifty baht a week, which was just under US$2.50. It wasn't a lot of money, but it was something, and I appreciated whatever I could get. Each morning I stood just inside the wire while he passed me clothes to sell. Jeans were the most popular items, especially stretch jeans. Sometimes my boss would return to the city to his real shop, leaving a couple of girls in his place. I got along very well with one of them, and she taught me more Thai in exchange for Chinese language lessons from me. The boss was half Chinese, so she figured it would be helpful for her to speak the language. Once again, I didn't have to worry about lunch. This was prepared everyday by the boss's wife and delivered to us. We actually became very busy. The more refugees who arrived from KID, the more customers we had. It helped that there was no shop on the other side of the road in the transit centre. People wanted to stock up on clothing before they left, worried they wouldn't have anything to wear when they reached their new countries. Eventually, my boss had to hire another boy as well. We were cheap labour. Our combined wage was less than half of what he paid to employ one girl.

There wasn't much to do after work. I would talk with the neighbours and reminisce about Phnom Penh in the old days. Aunt Keang often wandered around the camp day-dreaming, then she met one of her old neighbours from Phnom Penh.

The neighbour told Keang that her brother was alive in Australia. Apparently, he had left Cambodia before the arrival of the Khmer Rouge, and had recently put an advertisement in the Bangkok Chinese newspaper asking for information about Keang and the rest of his family.

Keang was not a very quick thinker after what she had gone through during Khmer Rouge, losing three children in a matter months. It did not even occur to her that this news could be our lifeline to escape from Phanat-Nikhom, but when Aunt Hun heard about it she quickly became excited.

"Who? Who was this neighbour?" she asked frantically.

We desperately needed a new sponsor if France refused to accept all of us, and Aunt Hun knew it was important to follow every potential lead. So Keang took Aunt Hun to see the old neighbour to get more information.

"I told you, your brother put in an advertisement wanting to hear if anyone knew about his missing relations," said the old neighbour.

It transpired that this had happened some months previously. Aunt Hun was like a terrier after a rat.

"What else did the ad say? What were the exact words? Do you remember his address? Do you still have the newspaper?"

Sadly, the neighbour could not remember any other details, nor had she kept the paper. Aunt Hun was very determined and rarely took no for answer. She thought through the night about that ad, and returned to the neighbour in the morning with more questions.

"Do you know the date of the ad? Could you remember what time of year?"

The best answer the neighbour could come up with was that it was towards the end of 1979[9]. Once again, Aunt Hun

---

[9] The true story about Cambodia genocide was exposed for the first time at the end of 1979 by an Australian journalist, John Pilger, on a British documentary, Year Zero: The Silent Death of Cambodia. It was reported that within two days of Year Zero going to air, 40 sacks of post arrived at ATV station in Birmingham - 26,000 first-class letters in the first post alone. The station quickly amassed £1m, almost all it in small amounts with a note: "This is for Cambodia".

had another sleepless night while she worked out what she could do next. Then, *voilà!* She remembered that when she was in Ho Chi Minh City, she had found the contact for her French professor through the Red Cross. Maybe she could do the same thing now. She went to see if they kept records of these kinds of ads - there were a lot of them at the time. Another month passed, but there was no news from the Red Cross. Aunt Hun was not to be put off, so she now wrote directly to the Bangkok Chinese newspaper.

"Dear Sir or Madam, I am looking for an ad placed by my brother, Ly Meng, around the end of 1979. He said he was looking for his family. I am now in Phanat-Nikhom Refugee Camp. Yours sincerely, Ly Keang."

The staff of the newspaper went above and beyond the call of duty. And the only reason that they recognised the names was because Aunt Hun had written to them in Chinese, using their Chinese names. Not only did they find the ad, they also got in contact with Keang's brother, who was now living in Sydney. They gave him Keang's address, and also arranged for a charity to come to the camp and deliver toothpaste, soap and other necessities to Small Uncle and Aunt Keang. Once more, we had hope. We casually nominated Australia in our refugee registration as our final destination, it was a dream away but now the dream was about to come true. I knew he wasn't a direct relation and I had never met him, but after all I was the kid who had got his sister out of KID. Surely that would mean something? The brother immediately lodged a sponsorship application - but in four names only: Small Uncle, Keang, Chou and Bim. Aunt Hun, Heng and Grandma were going to France. It seemed no one wanted Aunt Muy or her children - or me.

Fortunately, Aunt Hun once again swung into action. She wrote to Keang's brother, Meng, pointing out that his sister owed her current place in the camp to my efforts. She told him how I had made them the luckiest refugees in Thailand by getting them out of KID in just three days. She reminded them how I had come with Chou through the jungle. She told them how remarkable it was that although I was just a kid I had managed to persuade a UNHCR staff member to let his sister's family onto the bus. If it hadn't been for me they would still be without official status, possibly also without even food. Aunt Hun did not ask Meng to sponsor anyone else; she just laid out the facts. Meng had a kind heart - in the end he agreed to take us all. Once again, my heart burst with anticipation.

While Aunt Hun was writing to Meng, another possibility for my freedom had emerged. I had slowly come to know my boss and his wife. They were really fond of me and were beginning to think of me like I was a child of their own. They started to discuss the option of adopting me, as they had no son. They felt I would be a good person to eventually run the family business. One day, without warning, my boss invited me to visit their home. I gladly accepted and he smuggled me out of the camp, hiding me in the back of his van amongst the clothing. I felt lucky, because no one in the camp got out except those who were led across the road to the transit centre. I was taken to Chonburi city, and that night I had dinner with him, his wife and two daughters. I stayed overnight, sleeping peacefully, and next morning I went back to the camp and started work as normal. That evening, though, I was severely scolded by Small Uncle. I hadn't told anyone I was going out of the camp, and they had been very worried about me. I hadn't had time to let them know, but I understood their concern. Not only could something have happened to me, but if my absence had been noted by the Thai authorities, it might have put the whole family's position in jeopardy. That didn't account for what happened next, though. Small Uncle picked up one of the bamboo cylinders that were used to partition the family's sleeping space and smashed it across my forehead, right there in front of Grandma, in front of everyone. Luckily it was an old piece because rather than knocking me out it split apart. The blow was hard enough, though, to make me fall to the floor. I curled myself into a ball, feeling intense pain in my forehead. I was scared - Small Uncle was bigger than me, and was the only adult male in our group. It was also his brother-in-law who was sponsoring us, so none of my aunts wanted to upset him by intervening. The only sound I could hear was the little voice of Grandma begging him to stop. This only appeared to inflame him further.

"Get up! Get up!" he shouted at me. "You're only pretending. You're just acting. Get up or I'll give you another one!"

Gradually it dawned on him that the neighbours were watching the whole thing, and he backed down.

I stood up and glared at him, wishing I was big enough to fight him back. This was his display of gratitude after what I'd done for him. He may as well have kicked me in the guts.

The next morning when I went to work, my boss knew something was wrong.

"Hey *Ah-Di* (little boy) everything alright at home?"

I didn't say anything. I liked him; even Grandma could tell he wanted to adopt me, although my parents were still alive in Cambodia. We hadn't told him about them - he thought I was staying with my grandmother and other relatives because I was an orphan. I wanted to tell him, but didn't want to cause any trouble. If word got back to the authorities, it could affect our sponsorship application.

Once Ly Meng had sent through the necessary paperwork for our sponsorship, we were called into the Australian diplomatic office for an interview. Along with Aunt Hun we all went to see him. I was full of hope. This was nearly the last hurdle. Soon we would be on our way. I practiced my answers for the interview in English.

"What is your name?"
"My name is Huy Do."
"Where were you born?"
"I was born in Phnom Penh, Cambodia."
"When is your date of birth?"
"May 16, 1966. I am fifteen years old."

I memorised my date of birth and my other personal details. I was eager to show the officer I would not be a burden to Australia if I was accepted to live there. I would do anything and everything to be a good citizen. I wasn't the only one memorising a speech - we were all nervous and mindful of what we would be saying and how important it was to get it right. There would probably not be a second chance. All thirteen of us were standing in the office waiting for the interview. I happily thought to myself: *I will be going to live in Australia.*

The officer, Mr Hatchings, came in and started reading our papers. We stood there quietly. There were so many of us in the small room, the air began to get stuffy. It was hot and I was sweating. Hatchings examined our applications closely, quickly noting that Aunt Hun and Heng had already been accepted to go to France. He stared at us, and I could feel that something was wrong. Far from being hot, now it felt like a bucket of cold water was being poured over me. He started speaking, and confirmed my fears. Because I could understand English I knew straight away we were in trouble.

"I can't accept your application," Mr Hatchings uttered. Before he could give a full explanation, Aunt Hun shouted out in a knee-jerk reaction.

"What?"

"I can't accept your application, because you have arrived here under the protection of France," he repeated. "Australia can't take a refugee who's been accepted by another country." "I can only review your application if you have been rejected by the French," he added.

After so much, it seemed our family was going to be split apart by red tape, some going to France and some to Australia. After all we'd been through it didn't seem fair. Aunt Hun tried to explain the situation, saying that the original French sponsorship had only been for her and Heng, but since then more family members had arrived, none of whom had *bona fide* refugee status: adding that all eleven members who had arrived after Aunt Hun and Heng were not registered as refugees back in KID as by that time the Thai authorities had closed the border and shut the gate on new refugees. No matter what she said, Mr Hatchings wouldn't budge. Aunt Hun was upset by his response as he told us all to leave the room without being interviewed for resettlement. One by one we slowly walked out. Aunt Hun was the last to go, and turned back to Mr Hatchings, the look of determination I now knew so well all over her face.

"It's vital that Heng and I stay with our family," she told him. "You have no idea what we've been through and why it's important that we stay together. Can you promise me that if the French reject my application, you will definitely accept my application for Australia?"

Mr Hatchings was stunned.

"I have to ask. I can't risk getting rejected by the French and have no guarantee of acceptance elsewhere," she added.

It was a gamble - Aunt Hun knew that it would probably be easier to stick with things as they were, with four of us going to France and the rest to Australia. It wasn't her place to decide which country she should be sent to, she should be grateful she had somewhere to go at all. But for us it was important that we stay together, especially for Grandma. Hatchings still said nothing. I doubt he'd ever heard of a refugee refusing their original sponsorship in favour of a second one. That kind of thing just didn't happen. I suspect he had to think the answer through thoroughly before he replied. It was so quiet I could hear the flies buzzing against the wall. We had no idea what his response would be. Finally, he stood up and turned to Aunt Hun.

"OK," he told her. "Yes, if you come here with proof you've been rejected by the French I'll process your application for Australia, for you and your entire family."

It was still a gamble. Aunt Hun could not be certain Hatchings would keep his side of the bargain. Perhaps he had said that just to get her out of the office. We walked back to our quarters slowly, mulling over the situation. Should Aunt Hun risk her offer to be resettled in France so she had a chance to stay with us? The situation only became more confusing with the election that had just happened in France in May 1981. We heard that François Mitterand, leading the Social Democrats, had defeated the conservatives of Valéry Giscard d'Estaing to become the first socialist elected President of France. The news sent shockwaves through the Cambodian refugee community - we had lived under the worst kind of left wing government, and the last thing people wanted now was to be resettled in France. Adding fuel to the fire, America changed its policy and said it would accept any refugee rejected by the French. This action upset Monsieur Tricorno, who was a loyal French citizen. He believed that France was a better place than America so he made it his personal crusade not to reject any applications.

It was an overreaction from us, but an understandable one. The word socialism in Khmer sent shivers down our spines. What did we know about the difference between socialism in France and what we had suffered through under the Khmer Rouge? For us it was the Khmer Rouge in the streets of Paris. After all, this was the city where Pol Pot and so many other high ranking Khmer Rouge leaders had been educated about Marxism. It was the birthplace of Angkar as we had known it. There was no way we wanted to be heading back into the jaws of the Tiger we had just escaped from.

Meanwhile Aunt Hun was having trouble with Monsieur Tricorno. As usual, she spoke to him very directly.

"Please reject our application *s'il vous plaît.*"

"*Pardon? Pourquoi voudriez-vous que je fasse cela?*" (Why would you want me to do that?) asked Monsieur Tricorno.

"So, we can apply for resettlement to another country," answered Aunt Hun. You can imagine the look on Monsieur Tricorno's face. It was obvious his French pride had been hurt. The next thing he asked was, "Are you going to apply for resettlement in America?"

Aunt Hun told him she wasn't, but added, "If France is not going to resettle all thirteen of us then I need a rejection so we can apply to go somewhere else". It was a bold move, but Monsieur Tricorno wasn't going to buy into it.

"You and your sister; your mother and the little boy have all been accepted already. Once you get to France you can sponsor everyone else."

It was a possibility, but one that had no guarantee of success and which, even if it did work, would in all likelihood take a very long time. We would be stuck in the camp until Aunt Hun's residency status on the other side of the world was clarified. Aunt Hun pushed Monsieur Tricorno to commit to accepting all of us, but he wouldn't budge.

"I'm sorry, I am not going to reject your application and it is not possible to accept all thirteen of you. They'll have to wait."

"Wait?!" exclaimed Aunt Hun emotionally. "How long? Three years?! Four years?! No, it's impossible!"

Monsieur Tricorno was clearly uncomfortable with the confrontation.

"I need to go and talk to my colleagues in Bangkok. I don't have the authority to make this decision," he told Aunt Hun, who immediately wondered if it was just an excuse.

By now Aunt Hun was on the edge of breaking down, and fought to hold back the tears. I had already been in the camp five months, Aunt Hun and Heng had been here for nine, waiting another year or longer would be interminable. She came back to our quarters, and her voice trembled as she recounted her experience. She started crying with bitterness in those teardrops. She had tried so hard to keep us all together; it just didn't seem fair we would be split up because of a fickle change in international relations. Being Aunt Hun, though, she did not give up that easily.

Since arriving in the camp she and Heng had worked as interpreters for Father D'Agostino, a priest who worked for the Catholic Office for Emergency and Refugee Relief (COERR). Father D'Agostino was an influential figure within the camp and after hearing Hun's story and seeing her tears, he took her to Monsieur Bernard, a French teacher who was also responsible for assisting refugees to resettle in France. Father D'Agostino was like Aunt Hun - he spoke very directly.

"Bernard, go and tell your embassy either to reject them or accept all of them. Let them all to go to Paris or not to go to Paris."

Monsieur Bernard sat there like a little boy without a slightest idea but the only words that came out of his mouth were "*Oui, Oui,* Father."

Monsieur Bernard went with Aunt Hun to see Monsieur Tricorno the following morning and suggested it would be appropriate for him to make his mind up one way or the other. At this stage, Tricorno must have realised he was fighting a losing battle because without another word he took those two ID photos that Aunt Hun held, turned them over and stamped rejected on the back of them. It was over, *Au revoir* Paris.

It was now June 1981. It had now been more than a month since we had met with Mr Hatchings and Aunt Hun had taken the certainty of resettlement and gambled it against the chance of being sent to Australia with her family. She just had to hope that Hatchings would keep his word. We applied for a second interview, which we were eventually granted. Once again, the whole thirteen of us stood in the same small office waiting to hear our fate. Like last time, we had spent the night before nervously preparing answers to every conceivable question. Suddenly, an officer, the Australian Minister for Immigration and Ethnic Affairs who had chosen today of all days to visit the camp, walked right into the room. He spoke to Hatchings as if we were invisible. Our previous encounter had lasted less than five minutes, but because of this impromptu meeting we stood there for nearly half an hour before the two men shook hands, the minister left and Mr Hatchings finally turned his attention to us. Perhaps he was in a good mood, possibly he was in a hurry to go and have some beers with the minister, or maybe it was just our lucky day because he only asked a couple of questions before stamping ACCEPTED on our applications. We were told to have new photos taken for our visas - and that was that!

The long pain of our journey was nearly at an end. It was all the more amazing because I didn't even know where Australia was - I couldn't have found it on a map. I didn't know how far it was from Cambodia. I didn't know anything about it - how big it was, even what language was spoken there. I didn't care. I was flooded with both relief and excitement. It didn't matter if I was going to Australia or America. Their names both start with the letter A, so they must very close to each other: I am going to Australia.

Chapter Twenty Two

To The Land of Oz

Other refugees had set out on their journeys long before I had and were still sitting in camps waiting for news. Some were our neighbours, astounded that we were moving on so quickly. Speed was relative, of course, Aunt Hun and Heng had been in Phanat-Nikhom for nearly a year. Never-the-less we were now on our way to a life with opportunity, where we would be free to walk the streets, find education, obtain employment - all the things a non-refugee can do. We left Mr Hatchings' office as soon as we could in case he changed his mind. We went back to our quarters ready to pack what few belongings we had. Within a week, we had boarded the bus that took us over the road to the transit centre. It would have been quicker to walk, but no refugees were allowed outside the fence. I said goodbye to my Thai boss. He and his wife were sad to see me go, and gave me a pair of jeans, a shirt and a belt as a farewell gift. It was a kind gesture.

Late June 1981. After transferring to the transit centre, we underwent a full medical check: blood and urine tests, physical examinations and chest X-rays. After this we presumed we would soon be on our way to Australia, but fate had another card up its sleeve. Grandma was diagnosed with tuberculosis and needed treatment before we could proceed any further. We had come to the centre expecting a short stay, but now we had to wait until she was completely cured. So close, and still so far. No one could say how long it would take her to respond to the medication. Conditions in this camp were a lot better than KID, and of course we had full food rations, but it was frustrating because we were still stuck behind barbed wire. There was no school and I was quickly bored. After a day or two hanging around with my cousins I started looking for work - I was running out of money and needed something to do.

There was no market inside the transit centre, however,

there was a Thai restaurant offering food for the people who worked or volunteered there. I spoke to the manager, a Thai woman who was instantly impressed that I could speak five languages. She offered me a job as a waiter. It was a busy place, catering not only for those employed in the camp, but also workers from the UNHCR and Red Cross offices as well as those from the nearby hospital. After a few days, the manager let me know she was looking for someone to wash dishes, so I took Aunt Muy up there and she was given the position. Of course, the good thing about working in the food industry is the food, and I was given lunch and dinner every day. I was paid the standard wage, 50 baht (US$2.50) a week, not a huge amount, but certainly better than nothing, especially when you consider I had my meals there as well. It should have been a dream job.

One afternoon a group of foreign workers came to have lunch. As the only English speaker I was asked to serve them. I went to take their order, and amongst them was a young American who ordered an omelette with rice. This wasn't on the menu, and I didn't know what an omelette was. How could I? I had never been to a restaurant where you could order anything you liked. I was more used to other kinds of food: frogs, rats, snakes and damn *Pratoo*. With my limited English I tried to understand what he meant. It seemed an omelette was something like a fried egg on top of some rice, so this was the literal translation I gave the chef.

When I brought out the dish it was obviously wrong, and I was sent back to the kitchen with a new explanation: "stir fried vegetables with an egg on top of some rice." Of course, this wasn't right, either. We tried again: "a fried egg and vegetables with rice."

By this time most of his companions had finished eating, but he was adamant he still wanted an omelette. The chef, however, was having no more of it. He was furious, and walked quickly from the kitchen to talk to the customer directly. I could tell he was angry by the way he was stamping his feet, and grunting.

"What you want?" he asked in Thai, then in bad English.

"I just want an omelette with vegetables on top of rice," he was told.

The chef quickly clarified the order.

You want an omelette with rice, *Chaimay*? (is it?)"

"Yes."

Done. The chef walked back into the kitchen staring at me, waving his ladle, grunting angrily and cursing me in Thai. I had taken the wrong order, not once, not twice, but three times! He started swearing at me and making rude remarks about my mother. This really upset me so I swore back at him. The chef was also the husband of the manager, who came over and tried to calm us down. She told her husband to shut up and gave me some words of encouragement and compassion. I was too upset, though, and it wasn't fair I had to take his abuse and cursing about Mama. I took off my apron and threw it into the kitchen shouting out "Screw you!" in Thai. The chef threw something back at me, but I was already out the door so he missed. As I walked out of the restaurant I burst into tears. I cried like a little boy who has just lost his favourite toy. The manager called out to me, asking me to return, but she couldn't follow me because she had to mind the cash register. There was no turning back - and all because my pride had been hurt.

The argument had been so loud that everyone in the restaurant had heard it, including the foreign workers sitting with the omelette obsessed American. They had heard the sound of cooking utensils being thrown and the chef swearing at me. I was sitting on a low fence distraught that I had lost my new job with the money it offered, and its free food and bottles of Coke. I thought about going back and apologising, but I wasn't ready for that yet, although I had really left myself in a bad position, as I had no other means of earning money. As I sat there I became aware that someone had come over to me. She was an American nurse named Robin Bacci, and she had an offer for me: would I come and work at the hospital as an interpreter? She handed me a handkerchief and watched as I wiped my tears away. She took me back into the restaurant to introduce me to her group and told them what had happened. The manager wanted to me to keep working as a waiter, but I explained about the job offer, which also paid better. I would also have more opportunity to improve my English there. The restaurant manager was very disappointed that I was leaving. This was the only time I had made a mistake, and in some ways with my language skills I was four waiters in one. She took my arm, dragging me back towards the kitchen, but Robin took the other one and pulled the other way.

"No, he's coming to work with us," she said, not wanting me to stay in a place where people were rude to me.

My new workplace was the American Refugee Committee's Medical Project Outpatient Hospital, set up by a non-profit, non-sectarian group to provide humanitarian assistance to refugees. I worked as an interpreter for the doctors and nurses, helping them gather information from patients so they could diagnose and treat them. I kept a small notebook in which I wrote down medical terminology and I soon built up a reputation for reliability and accuracy. I was well known and well liked not just by the medical staff, but by the Thai ambulance drivers and even the camp guards, who quickly got used to me waving my ARC ID badge at them whenever I entered or left the camp. After three months, I was given a new role: assistant to the field coordinator. Her name was Sandee Evenson, a nurse who supervised thirty-five refugee staff working in the outpatient department. I managed the transport service that ran between our hospital and the one run in the processing camp, and also oversaw the placement of patients in the wards, making sure they were in the right place for treatment and testing.

One early morning, while everyone was still in bed, a little boy came knocking on the hospital door. It was an emergency - his mother was about to give birth, and she was too far away to walk. I woke the duty ambulance driver and we went and picked her up. She was in a lot of pain. Kids followed us back to the hospital, wondering what would happen to her. We made it inside the front doors and I had her rest on one of the benches while I ran for help. When I returned with Dr Longfils she was lying down. Her waters had broken and she was looking extremely lethargic. The baby was about to arrive, so the hospital staff carried her into a nearby room. I had to remain with her so I could interpret for her, but first I had to chase the kids away. They stood at the door, and then at a window, until I drew the curtain. I was there for the whole thing, though, the first time I had seen a baby born. I felt very privileged to be part of such an experienced team.

The medical staff were mainly from America, but there were also Australians, Belgians and Japanese. I was unique among them, in that I knew both worlds, the world of the camp and the world of the inner workings of the hospital. Working at the hospital was more interesting than anything else I had ever done, and during the three months we waited for Grandma to get well, I spent most of my time in the wards. I was even allocated a room to stay in the hospital overnight, although a nightshift worker used the bed during the day. I learned many things watching the doctors and nurses, but one day Dr Longfils, a grumpy doctor from Belgium, learned a new medical procedure from me. An injured boy had been carried in by his father - he had a large cut just above his Achilles tendon. The father had put on a rough bandage which Dr Longfils now cut off. He was surprised to see a bundle of old leaves fall out of it. I told him it was tobacco. He said he knew what it was, but didn't know why it was there. I explained that we used the leaves to stop blood flowing from a wound, and also because they had antiseptic properties. The look on his face was priceless: he must have thought we were crazy. He cleaned the wound and put on a bandage, good naturedly teasing me in front of the other doctors. I thought of telling him how rabbit poo had cured my malaria… or how coconut oil had made my hair grow as a baby. I didn't mind that he was amused - the hospital was a great place to be, and I was friends with adults who respected me. I was so happy there I sometimes even forgot I was a refugee!

Eventually Grandma's tuberculosis was cured and in early

October we were told that the Australian embassy was ready to issue our travel documents. On the fifth I was finally issued with my visa. It was an emotional time for me as I made the rounds of the hospital saying goodbye to my friends and colleagues. I made sure I thanked Robin Bacci, the nurse who had shown so much belief in me that I had gotten the job in the first place. One of the other nurses, Nancy Johansen, gave me *The Adventures of Tom Sawyer* as a souvenir. I still have it. In the front, she wrote: "Do Huy - good luck in the future. I hope you will get some enjoyment out of this book! Take care - Love Nancy." Maybe it doesn't sound like much, but I had rarely ever received any gifts - and certainly not in either the labour camp nor the refugee camps. I also received two references from the Field Coordinators, one from Sandee Evenson and the second from Scott Brady - a young man with a preference for omelettes!

The next day I packed my few belongings - my book, some photos and a few clothes - into my *Krama* and climbed aboard the waiting coach. All thirteen of us were on the bus. Somehow, we had achieved the impossible.

Small Uncle and Keang and their children were a few rows behind me. Without me they might still be in KID - but without Keang's brother I might still be in the processing camp. Small Uncle hadn't apologised for beating me - or thanked me for getting him out of KID, for that matter - but nevertheless he was my father's brother - my uncle. As such, he was family, and I wasn't about to disown him. With all the excitement and relief rushing through my entire body I wasn't dwelling on the past, anyway, and I was thinking about what lay ahead of me in Australia. The coach pulled up and it was raining heavily as I leaped from the bus to hotel we were staying in overnight. I didn't even bother to take my belongings with me - what was the point? I wouldn't need them overnight

The next morning, we were driven through Bangkok en route to the airport. I had forgotten what a busy city looked like - it had been six years since the fall of Phnom Penh, and I supposed I had forgotten many other normal things in that time as well. The streets were full of hawkers and motorbikes. The traffic was so bad the coach could hardly move. It took us two hours to reach the airport and the plane that was waiting to take us to our new home, Thai Airlines Flight TG983. It started to hit me then: we had finally done it, I had finally escaped. I was leaving the Khmer Rouge, refugee camps, everything. I was about to take my first plane trip. We were given seats at the rear of the plane, there were some other refugee families there already. The jet engines were so loud I could hardly hear people talking, even the flight attendant's instructions. My heart was full and I couldn't talk as the plane started to rumble down the runway. This was it! I was leaving Asia but I still didn't know where was Australia. It had been more than a year since Mama had hugged me out the front of our tiny hut, twelve months since Father had spoken his words of advice. After I ate my dinner, amazingly, I fell asleep until I was woken by the sun coming through the window. At approximately 7:30 in the morning of Thursday October 8, 1981, we touched down at Sydney's Kingsford Smith airport. Thirteen members of the Do's family finally resettled in a new land of Australia. One by one, we stepped out of the plane and proceeded toward the special immigration section for refugees. Australia has a few nicknames. Some people call it the sunburnt country; others call it the land down under. The freckled face red haired customs woman spoke an unfamiliar dialect of English.

"G'day mate, welcome to Oz! Where you're from?" She asked with a smile.

I smiled back, wondering what she meant. She had spoken so fast I had barely understood her. Obviously, she could tell where I have come from: a refugee camp! I moved on as she called for the next number. As we progressed through customs and immigration and beyond, I soon learned it was very important to insert two important words into my English sentences as often as possible. I heard what the lady said to me.

"Once you're done with the immigration, *you know*, there's a coach waiting outside, *you know*, to take all of you to the centre in Villawood, *you know*, your temporary home, *you know*."

I was happy to be there. While waiting in the last camp we had been shown films of Australia so I had some idea of what to expect. I had seen wide, empty tree-lined roads devoid of people and full of parked cars. It looked so beautiful and peaceful. Tall trees stood along both sides of the road in full blossom, vivid purple flowers standing out against an unfamiliar clear blue sky. These were trees with names that I could not pronounce: jacarandas and eucalyptus trees.

Someone had shown me a map of the world, so at least I understood why they said, "down under." Six months ago, I had never heard of it - now I was about to spend my first night here. It took us about forty-five minutes to reach the hostel just before lunch time. There were other immigrants with us, some from Cambodia but others from Vietnam and Laos. Of course, I quickly found myself translating for people. We were given small units to stay in - I was placed with Aunt Hun, Heng and Grandma. For the first time in my life I had a room of my own. That night I lay there in the dark, staring at the faint white ceiling: *I missed my family, my brothers, my father, and especially my mother.*

I missed the way she moved and the authority in her voice. She never had to say, "I am the boss of this household," but all of us, even my father, always obeyed her. I missed her stubbornness, her determination and her confidence. She seemed to know everything and anything. She often said with a smile from the corner of her mouth, "I know everything. You can't hide anything from me."

My younger brothers and I would giggle and tell her, "Sure Mama, you know nothing."

Whether she knew everything or nothing, it was her confidence and her maternal instinct that kept all of us alive under the Khmer Rouge. Amongst my feelings of elation and relief I also felt guilt at having left my family behind. Here I was in my own room in a comfortable bed, while back in Phnom Penh they still suffered. They were still trapped, although I was finally free.

I would bring them here. I vowed that somehow, they, too, would know these feelings of relief, of safety and of opportunity. They, too, would know what it felt like to find sanctuary.

Khao-I-Dang, Thailand, 1980. With a neighbour and my precious orange checked shirt.

Phanat-Nikhom June 1981: Left to right Aunt Muy's children, Bim (being held by her mother, Keang), Aunt Keang, Small Uncle (Chou in front), Grandma Lee, Me, Muy, Hun and Heng.

Epilogue

A decade after the Khmer Rouge and Pol Pot were ousted, guerrilla warfare continued along the Cambodian border and eventually spilled into Thailand. The United Nations General Assembly continued to recognise the Khmer Rouge as the legitimate government of Cambodia - Democratic Kampuchea into the 80s. Australia, my new home, played a major role in bringing peace and stability to Cambodia today. The former Australian Foreign Minister, Dr Gareth Evans, presented the Cambodian Peace Plan at the Jakarta Meeting in 1989. The aim was to bring about a ceasefire, and the first ever deployment of a United Nations peacekeeping force to oversee the country until the establishment of a nationally elected government. The First Paris Conference on Cambodia was held but failed to obtain a peace agreement for the children and people of Cambodia. In that same year, on the 26th September, 1989, the Vietnamese occupation of Cambodia officially ended and the remaining troops withdrew. Eventually, an agreement known as the Paris Peace Accord was signed on the 23rd October, 1991, by the Coalition Government of Democratic Kampuchea. Ironically the coalition government was not the one in power governing Cambodia at the time nor were they the ones who had and liberated me from the Khmer Rouge Labour camp.

The Khao-I-Dang Refugee Camp was opened in November 1979 and formally closed in 1992 under the United Nations Transitional Authority in Cambodia (UNTAC) repatriation program to clear the way for Cambodian Election in 1994. In April 1992, more than a quarter of million Cambodian refugees, who were still stuck in camps along the Thai-Cambodian borders over a decade after the fall of Khmer Rouge regime, were repatriated into Cambodian territory under the arrangement and protection of UNTAC. During my last visit to Phnom Penh in 2008, I made an effort to visit my old house at Kandal Market again but they were still destroyed including the Pepsi Cola factory behind our house.

Uncle Yu now lives in my old hut at Kilo 4 along with his wife and three children. He has been making a living from selling daily necessities: everything from chewing gum to cigarettes, gasoline and natural gas.

Aunt Hiam also moved back to Phnom Penh with her two children after her first husband died. She struggled to make a living on the streets of Phnom Penh and later married a Khmer cyclo-rickshaw driver. She had two more children with him and now works as a cleaner earning about USD2.00 a day, barely enough to make ends meet. Although Cambodia is slowly and gradually recovering from the nightmare of the Khmer Rouge, many Cambodians still live below the poverty line, especially those in the rural areas.

In August, 1985, my parents and four brothers had made their long and dangerous journey across the Thai-Cambodian borders to Khao-I-Dang Refugee Camp on the same route as that I took five years earlier. Seven years after I left home, in March 16, 1987, my family was finally accepted by the Australian Government under the Special Programme for Humanitarian Aid and I was, at last, reunited with my parents and brothers - including two more who had been born in Khao-I-Dang Refugee Camp.

2017 marked the thirtieth anniversary of my reunion with my family and their resettlement in Australia, however, I'll never forget the day when I was still a little boy and those young Khmer Rouge revolutionaries ordered us out of our home, grandly promising, "You can come back soon, in a few days. Maybe tomorrow". How many never came back. And, of course, the images, memories of Cambodian genocide and the brutality of the Khmer Rouge remain vividly clear - as they do in the minds and hearts of so many survivors.

Acknowledgements

I would like to express my sincere and deepest gratitude to my friends, Allison Baker, Graham Street, Ming Woo, and my editor, Simon Luckhurst, for their comments and feedbacks to make my memoir a reality. Without their help, this story would still be just another notebook. It was because of their assistance and encouragement, I can put my story together for the future generations to read and learn from history.

My history.

About the Author

Vincent Lee (Chinese name: 李騰輝 *Lee Teng Huy*) was born and grew up in Phnom Penh, Cambodia. Vincent's parents were both ethnic Chinese-Cambodian. Like many of his Cambodian generation, from April 17, 1975, when the Pol Pot's Khmer Rouge seized control of Phnom Penh, Vincent was taken away from his family at the age of ten to join a labour camp for boys and endured four years of brutality and starvation. Vincent was one of the luckiest survivors of the greatest genocide in Cambodian history under the regime.

In 1980, Vincent escaped with his Grandmother, risking his life across Cambodia jungle of landmines into the refugee camp in Thailand. Vincent arrived in Sydney, Australia, in 1981 under the Refugee and Special Humanitarian Program.

In 1982 at the age of eighteen, he began sustained formal education for the first time at the Christian Brother's school in Sydney. He cleaned classrooms and worked at night to pay his school fees, and combined works and studies to complete his degree at Sydney University in 1991. He also holds a master degree in Finance from the University of Technology, Sydney.

www.ingramcontent.com/pod-product-compliance
Lightning Source LLC
Chambersburg PA
CBHW070604300426
44113CB00010B/1400